FLY FISHING
Southern
COLORADO

FLY FISHING
Southern
COLORADO

AN ANGLER'S GUIDE

Craig Martin, Tom Knopick,
John Flick

PRUETT

PRUETT PUBLISHING COMPANY
BOULDER, COLORADO

Printed in the United States

10 9 8 7 6 5 4 3 2 1

Library of Congress Cataloging-in-Publication data

Martin, Craig, 1952–
    Fly fishing southern Colorado : an angler's guide / Craig Martin,
Tom Knopick, John Flick.
        p.   cm.
    Includes index.
    ISBN 0-87108-872-X (pb)
    1. Trout fishing—Colorado—Guidebooks. 2. Fly fishing—Colorado—
Guidebooks. 3. Colorado—Guidebooks. I. Knopick, Tom, 1956– .
II. Flick, John, 1956– . III. Title.
SH688.U6M37   1996
799.1'755—DC20   96-44765
                                                                CIP

Cover and book design by Jody Chapel, Cover to Cover Design
Cover photograph by Craig Martin
Book composition by Lyn Chaffee
Maps by Craig Martin

CONTENTS

PREFACE

To my mind, few endeavors in life are more exciting than exploring a new location. The guise of the adventure doesn't matter. Give me a topographic map or a secondhand story about some wonderful spot and I'll grab a mountain bike, a rucksack, or a fly rod and be off. The attraction lies in anticipation of what might lie beyond the boundaries of where I've been. Will the next bend in the river reveal to me the perfect crystal pool hiding a beautiful brook trout? After peeling away the outer trappings, this is the same attraction as that of fly fishing itself: the chance that each drift may bring a trout to the fly. In essence, every cast explores unknown territory.

And so when my first guidebook, *Fly Fishing in Northern New Mexico* (written with the Sangre de Cristo Fly Fishers), was completed in 1991, I was searching for new territory. In the previous year and a half I'd looked at about forty streams and lakes around New Mexico and found dozens of delightful spots. Although the Sangre de Cristo Mountains held more than a few unexplored streams, my imagination was drawn north of the border, to the mountains of Colorado. I'd driven through the San Juan Mountains dozens of times on my way to hike a trail or ride a single track, but I never stopped to test the waters. When I finally made my first trip to the Conejos River, I got lucky and landed a brown trout as long as my forearm. I was hooked. The San Juans reeled me in, and I didn't put up much of a fight.

A couple years later I met Tom Knopick at a fly-fishing gathering in Santa Fe. Tom teased the group with a bit of his knowledge about the waters around Durango, and suddenly my interest in southern Colorado fishing leaped over the Continental Divide. I started mulling the possibilities for another guidebook. Between us, Tom and I could cover the region. In late 1994, Tom, his business partner John Flick, and I began our collaboration on this book.

Working with Tom and John is a pleasure. The two have been in the fly-fishing business together since 1983 as owners of Duranglers Flies and Supplies in Durango. They know the San Juans intimately, and the details of their knowledge was a constant amazement to me. I'd mention a little hole on the Piedra River where I'd found a nice fish, and they knew which rock I was talking about. As we began work, I was secretly thrilled that they treated me as an equal, for these two gentlemen are superb fly fishermen for which my modest abilities are no match.

After three years of researching mountain bike and hiking guides, it was a pleasure to have the excuse to go fly fishing every week. Although my family—June, Jessica, and Alex—grew tired of the drive north from Los Alamos to Pagosa Springs, they never complained about our weekends along the streams of the San Juans. The summer we spent field-checking details for this book was wonderful—filled with fine hikes, inspiring scenery, and many special moments. Most memorable was the dawning of a love of fly fishing in my children. On a backpack trip along the Los Pinos River, daughter Jessica caught her first trout on a fly rod, then carefully released the brookie back to the water, grinning the whole time. Her wide eyes told me she was on her way to becoming a fly fisher. Young Alex can't yet swing a rod, but he always asked to touch my catches, proudly dipping his hands in the water to wet them before gingerly placing the tip of his index finger on the fish.

Guidebooks are never written solely by their authors, and I would be remiss not to extend my thanks to the many anonymous public servants with the United States Forest Service (USFS), the Bureau of Land Management (BLM), and the Colorado Department of Wildlife (CDOW) who patiently answered my questions about facilities, policies, and management practices. John Alves of the CDOW in Monte Vista was particularly helpful in supplying information about trout species, stocking patterns, and whirling disease.

Entomologist B. C. Kondratieff of Colorado State University graciously reviewed the aquatic insect list and made numerous corrections that made the list more accurate. Thanks also to Donald Cutter, retired professor of history at the University of New Mexico, for sharing his extensive knowledge of the Juan Rivera expedition of 1765, confirming my suspicion that many of the rivers draining the San Juans to the south were named by this little-known Spanish explorer.

Special thanks to my friend and frequent fishing partner Kevin Ott for sharing fine days, frustrating days, and rain-soaked days on the Rio Grande, the Conejos, the Dolores, and the Piedra. I'm especially grateful that he didn't shove me into the runoff-swollen Rio Grande when I told him about my plans to include some of our favorite places in this book.

The most striking contrast between New Mexico and Colorado angling is not the size of the rivers or the beauty of the surrounding mountains but the sheer number of streams. In New Mexico, any stream you can cross in three steps is called a river, and even those are few in number. After years of living in the high desert, I've developed a fondness for such intimate waters. In Colorado, every valley lying between two hills lights up with sparkling water, surely the home of a few spotted trout. I've ignored such places to adequately cover the major rivers for this book. Even after spending three summers there, the song of the San Juans continues to ring in my ears, calling me to return to those hundreds of unexplored little streams.

1

FLY FISHING
IN SOUTHERN COLORADO:

An Introduction

Fly fishing has as much to do with ragged purple mountaintops, water cascading over rounded boulders in steep-walled canyons of pink granite, and sunlight streaming through Douglas firs as it does with fish. In pursuit of trout, anglers find themselves in some of the world's loveliest places and perhaps, either knowingly or subconsciously, derive as much satisfaction from simply entering the trout's environment as they do from catching their quarry. Angling carries no guarantee of success, and more often than not a cast to a stream or lake results in failure. Yet anglers continue to head for the water because the places trout live are as important to them as are the speckled fish.

The highest order of trout place is an unclouded mountain stream tumbling through a boulder-strewn canyon with stately snowcapped peaks occasionally glimpsed through the trees. Such a scene, with the addition of a fat cutthroat trout sipping a mayfly from the glassy surface, is the essence of angling in southern Colorado.

As the popularity of fly fishing grows along with the need to escape the hectic circles of our everyday lives, more fishermen are taking to the rivers. Angling need not always be about crowded rivers where other fishermen are never out of sight. The mountains of southern Colorado are tucked away in a remote corner of the state, far removed from large cities. A few popular spots in the area may seem crowded, but for those willing to hoof it, even for as little as a quarter-mile, the streams of the San Juan Mountains offer some old-fashioned have-the-river-to-yourself fly fishing. Rest assured that even the angler who desires roadside fishing can find idyllic places to cast his flies, but the bit of extra effort required to remove oneself from the road pays ample rewards.

Like the sport of fly fishing itself, this out-of-the-way portion of Colorado is gradually being discovered by people who seek to break from their routines. Little effort is required to find a more peaceful spot to spend a couple of hours. Southern Colorado has scenery, the chance for solitude, and a multitude of special places where one can become immersed in the landscape. And it delivers in another way: The streams draining the San Juan Mountains hold fine populations of trout that can give an angler a day on the water he or she will never forget.

The Lay of the Land

Although the majority of Colorado was settled from the north and east, the southern quarter of the state was settled from the south. The main chain of the Rockies, and the San Juans themselves, were a formidable barrier to travel from the cities of the East, Midwest, and even from Denver in the early days of the Colorado territory. Access to suitable land for settlements, farming, and ranching was limited to torturous trails entering the lands of the Utes from the south.

The first Europeans to explore this remote corner of what was to become Colorado were Spanish soldiers and friars working out of the New Mexican towns of Santa Fe and Taos. A glance at a map makes this point obvious. Towns and rivers of this corner of Colorado carry lilting Spanish names: San Juan, Dolores, Vallecito, Hermosa, Animas, Florida.

Many of the geographic features of the region—including most of the rivers—were named in the 1760s by Spanish explorer Juan Rivera. Heading north and west from Santa Fe in search of silver and gold ores, Rivera passed from the vicinity of Chama, New Mexico, to Durango and then on to Dolores before turning northward to reach the Gunnison River. Along the way, his journal often includes a description of a newly discovered river or mountain peak, then states, "We gave it the name . . ." Sometimes Rivera simply translated the Ute names for rivers into Spanish, but he frequently ascribed his impressions to the land. The names Rivera gave to Colorado rivers might have been lost had it not been for two members of his party who accompanied the friars Atanasio Dominguez and Silvestre Velez de Escalante on their famous trip along the same basic route eleven years later. The guides passed on the names given to features by Rivera, thus attaching them forever to the landscape.

Southwest Colorado is a land of transition. The lofty ranges that create its serrated skyline are a part of the Rocky Mountains, the chain of peaks that runs north through Wyoming and Montana to Canada. But the affinities of the surrounding rocks, of the vegetation, and of the climate clearly link this portion of Colorado to the nearby southwestern deserts. Banded horizontal sandstone flanks the mountains to the south; piñon, agave, and low mats of cactus grow in the foothills; and most days bring shining blue skies and low humidity. Caught between the two worlds—dizzying mountains and shimmering deserts—southern Colorado enjoys the benefits and beauties of both.

Southern Colorado is dominated by the peaks of the majestic San Juan Mountains, and the region is sometimes called the "Switzerland of America." From the pancake-flat San Luis Valley on the east to the canyon of the Dolores River near the Utah border, the scenery of the region is magnificent.

The eastern edge of the San Juan Mountains rises from the parklike San Luis Valley, a vast basin the size of Connecticut that is ringed with mountains. The Rio Grande flows slowly across the valley, then dives into New Mexico. Ragged

The thin-layered sandstone of the Dolores River Canyon shows the link between the San Juan Mountains and the southwestern deserts. (Photograph by Kevin Ott.)

cliffs are characteristic of the eastern half of the San Juans, which are not much more than an immense pile of volcanic rocks. At least fifteen massive explosive volcanoes were active in the region during the Miocene period, around 25 million years ago. Their monumental eruptions covered the landscape with thousands of feet of ash and volcanic debris. Today, brown-and-purple cliffs common in the eastern San Juans mark the location of these volcanic deposits.

The western portion of the range is composed of sharp-ridged mountains made of ancient metamorphic rocks shoved by tectonic forces from below sea level to their current position. Many peaks reach above 14,000 feet, and summits over 12,000 feet are too numerous to count.

To the west of the mountains lie the deserts of the Colorado Plateau and the Great Basin. The first barrier to moisture moving in from the Pacific Ocean is the imposing crest of the San Juans. As a result, precipitation falls freely in summer and winter, creating an island of forest amid the normally dry high desert. The valleys radiating from the peaks were once filled with glaciers. Now, cascading streams drop from the ridges and gather into larger rivers, the places where anglers find paradise. Eventually, these rivers leave the mountains and are collected by the San Juan River to the south, the Colorado River to the north, and the Rio Grande to the east.

A winter's worth of snow can accumulate to depths of twenty or more feet in the wetter parts of the range. Such a snowpack creates a tremendous amount of water that must drain out of the mountains in spring. As a result, runoff in the San Juans is frequently long and heavy. Yet the affiliation with the southwestern deserts is strong, and winters with below-normal snowpack are common. The ensuing springs can bring runoff that comes and goes in several weeks, opening up a long summer of angling.

Each winter brings a unique set of snow conditions that lead to a wide range of runoff timing and circumstances. Depending on the snowpack, spring temperatures, and size and elevation of the watershed, high water may range from early June to mid-July. In most years, runoff winds down from mid- to late June. Runoff in the eastern volcanic mountains is often discolored, but high flows in the streams draining the central metamorphic range remain clearer. On the Animas River, the red Mesozoic sediments in the Hermosa Cliffs can turn runoff into a muddy mess for a short period of time.

Compensation for spring runoff reaches anglers in the fall. Due to the mountains' southern latitude and the mild climate they bring to the lower elevations, autumn is a favorite time for many southern Colorado anglers. Crisp blue skies, chilly mornings, and warm afternoons greet anglers who can read-just their thinking to the fantastic fall conditions that southern Colorado offers. Low, clear water is found in all the major streams. Water temperatures warm by late morning, and sparse but effective hatches can occur until winter arrives, or beyond. During most years, anglers can fish comfortably into November or even December. Another powerful attraction of the fall is the increased activity of brown trout.

The San Juan environment offers anglers much more than the opportunity to fool plenty of trout. Every trout stream is a natural cathedral. The beauty of the mountains everywhere will cause you to stop and stare, often in the middle of a cast. On days when the fish seem to be buried in the gravel and nothing will bring them to your fly, you can still return home feeling refreshed.

Trout of Southern Colorado

Rainbow trout are the most widespread salmonid in the wa-ters of southern Colorado. Long the mainstay of stocking pro-grams throughout the state, rainbows adapt well to a wide range of environmental conditions and thus are found in streams and lakes from the lowlands up to 12,000 feet. The popularity of the species stems from its ability to give the angler a battle when hooked. Rainbows are strong and showy fighters, often leaping from the water in an effort to shake the hook. Rainbows feed aggressively, which helps them grow quickly in rich stream habitats. Anglers will find most rainbows ranging from 7 to 20 inches, with large fish weighing over four pounds. In many streams, 12- to 14-inch rainbows are common.

Not all rainbows found in Colorado are fresh from the hatchery. Several rivers, notably the Rio Grande and the Animas, have been planted with wild strains of rainbows. These superior fish provide the angler with a more challenging, healthier trout and are often protected by special regulations to help insure their continuance as a population. In many places in almost all watersheds in the San Juan Mountains, rainbow populations have become self-sustaining.

One possibly frightening characteristic of the rainbow trout is its susceptibility to whirling disease. The protozoan parasite responsible for the disease attacks developing cartilage and can deform fish or cause severe nerve damage that makes affected individuals chase their tails, swimming in circles. Rainbow trout populations in heavily infected waters can be decimated; lightly infected waters may show no signs of strain. Spores, in effect the eggs of the protozoan, can live in river silt or even dry mud for thirty years. Mud picked up on waders in one stream can carry the disease to another watershed. Anglers can help prevent the spread of the disease by frequently cleaning their waders and wading shoes.

Thus far in southwestern Colorado, whirling disease is known only from a few waters, most notably the upper Rio Grande. The Colorado Department of Wildlife previously assumed that whirling disease was a hatchery problem that would not disrupt wild trout populations and has continued stocking infected hatchery fish in certain waters known to contain the disease.

Brown trout are the most common wild trout in the lower elevation streams and rivers of southern Colorado. Some stocking of brown trout continues, but most populations are

self-sustaining and have been for decades. Browns can tolerate higher water temperatures than rainbows, cutthroats, and
brook trout and so thrive in the lower reaches of mountain
streams and rivers, particularly in the Animas River. Browns
are not generally found above 10,000 feet. In small streams
browns can average 10 or 12 inches, and in large rivers four-
pound browns ply the deep water like miniature submarines.

Brown trout will feed actively on adult insects and thus
readily take dry flies. Browns aggressively take caddisflies and
stoneflies and are known for their fondness for terrestrials,
particularly grasshoppers. In the Animas River brown trout
show their predatory nature and are sustained by the river's
large sculpin population. In mountain streams browns range
from 7 to 18 inches, with larger fish occasionally taken in the
Animas. Browns do much of their feeding early and late in the
day, and large browns often feed at night.

Anglers often speak of "wily browns," and with good rea-
son. These trout are not known for a flashy fight but are more
likely to challenge the angler with an upstream run, a leap
over a boulder, or a charge into a submerged tangle of
branches and roots. Landing a wild brown trout in a mountain
stream or river is one of the supreme challenges and joys of
fly fishing.

The non-native brook trout is plentiful in many streams
and lakes in the San Juan Mountains. Once a significant part
of stocking programs throughout the west, brook trout are
now stocked only in a few lakes and streams. Most brookies in
southern Colorado are wild fish, descendants of fish stocked
over twenty years ago. Brookies are perhaps the most exquis-
itely colored trout, with green backs, orange undersides, and
flashes of red and yellow on the flanks. Brook trout populations thrive in the upper reaches of most streams and in timberline lakes. Their inability to tolerate water temperatures
above 75 degrees makes brookies a backcountry fish. They
are opportunistic feeders, taking almost any well-presented fly
that floats by. Brook trout remain small, and anglers will find

This hefty brown trout pulled from the Rio Grande thought a bright orange Stimulator was a meaty salmon fly. (Photograph by Craig Martin.)

most of them under 8 inches; a good brook trout is 11 inches or better. In some lakes, however, brookies can reach over 15 inches, and some of these fish may weigh up to three pounds.

Two subspecies of native trout are found in southern Colorado. East of the Continental Divide, in waters that drain into the Gulf of Mexico, Rio Grande cutthroats are found. Over the passes on the west side of the Divide, Colorado River cutthroats are native. Both subspecies survive in a range that is much reduced when compared to their distribution at the beginning of the twentieth century. Colorado River cutthroats once swam large and small rivers from Utah and Wyoming into Arizona and the San Juan drainage in New Mexico. The waters of the Rio Grande drainage were home to Rio Grande cutthroats. Competition and hybridization with introduced trout, heavy metal contamination from mining operations, and habitat destruction have all served to push cutthroats back into smaller headwater streams. Only a few pure populations are found in southern Colorado.

Both native cutthroat species are attractive fish washed in orange and with constellations of large black spots concentrated near the tail. Like all high-elevation trout, they are opportunistic feeders, taking mostly aquatic and terrestrial insects. Colorado River cutthroats tend toward streams with a good percentage of quiet water. Rio Grande cutthroats inhabit either quiet water or riffles and runs. Because of their nutrient-poor habitat, most cutthroats are small, ranging from 5 to 7 inches. In secluded mountain streams a good cutthroat might measure up to 14 inches.

Colorado River and Rio Grande cutthroats hold but a tenuous grasp on their survival. Special regulations protect native populations on the East Fork of Hermosa Creek and the Lake Fork of the Conejos. Because of their sensitivity to angling pressure, we encourage anglers to treat all native cutthroat waters as catch-and-release.

Several non-native subspecies of cutthroat have been or continue to be stocked in southern Colorado waters. Snake River and Yellowstone strains were planted in many drainages in the last fifty years, but most stocking programs for these fish were halted a decade ago. Pure-strain cutthroats, both native and non-native, are rarely found; most individuals exhibit some degree of hybridization with rainbow trout. Cutbow hybrids are common in many watersheds.

Towns and Services

Southern Colorado is delightfully isolated from large population centers: To the north and east, Denver is 300 miles from the Conejos River; to the south, Albuquerque is 200 miles away. But the San Juans aren't exactly the boondocks. Towns, both large and small, and villages surround the mountains and offer anglers a wide variety of services and some of the comforts of home.

Durango is the largest town in the San Juans, with a population around twelve thousand. Centrally located, Durango offers a wide variety of activities to the outdoor enthusiast. Mountain biking, horseback riding, river rafting, hiking, skiing, and, of course, fishing are all part of the Durango scene. It's the kind of town where you might overhear a grizzled angler state, "My favorite spot for brown trout is on the Animas, right behind the mall." In addition, many family attractions are located here and nearby, such as the Durango and Silverton Narrow Gauge Railroad and Mesa Verde National Park.

As the major supply center of the San Juans, Durango offers just about everything. Visitors will find a wide range of services to suit all tastes and budgets. The town boasts dozens of motels and service stations, restaurants from fast food to fancy, and a growing number of microbreweries. Several chain grocery and discount stores take care of most of your basic needs for food and camping supplies. Full-service fly-fishing shops and several guide services are also available. If you can't find it in Durango, you should have brought it with you.

A number of midsized towns also offer visitor services. These towns have a small selection of lodging, local restaurants, service stations, and often a large chain grocery store. Not everything you might need will be available in these places, but you should be able to find most of what you desire. Pagosa Springs, Del Norte, Monte Vista, and Alamosa each offer these kinds of facilities. Of these, Pagosa Springs is the most tourist-oriented town, and anglers will find a fly-fishing shop on Main Street.

Creede, Dolores, Antonito, South Fork, and Bayfield are small towns that offer visitors basic services with limited choices. Stop into these towns to get the basics.

Camping

Private campgrounds are found near all towns in southern Colorado. Usually along the main roads, these establishments provide water, sewers, electric hookups, showers, and often recreational facilities. The developed area around Vallecito Lake also offers full-service RV parks.

Forest Service campgrounds are located throughout Rio Grande and San Juan National Forests. Most rivers and large lakes have campgrounds nearby, and their locations are pointed out in the chapters to follow. Sites are usually well spaced and wooded. Most Forest Service campgrounds have water and pit toilets and charge a small fee.

Primitive camping is permitted along many forest roads. Before selecting a spot to pitch your tent, check at the ranger station to find areas where dispersed camping is permitted. This style of camping offers more solitude and scenery but comes with some additional responsibilities. To avoid additional damage to an already overtaxed landscape, select a site that shows signs of previous use. Use existing fire rings. Pack out all your trash and bury all human waste at least two hundred feet from streams and lakes. Don't forget to bring your own water.

Land Management

Rio Grande and San Juan National Forests hold the majority of acreage in the mountains of southern Colorado and consequently manage the land surrounding many of the trout streams and lakes. The forests are comanaged as a single unit. Rio Grande National Forest encompasses the eastern half of the San Juans, including the watersheds of the Rio Grande and Conejos Rivers. On the other side of the Continental Divide, San Juan National Forest encompasses the San Juan, Piedra, Los Pinos, Animas, La Plata, and Dolores watersheds. For more information, contact the Forest Supervisor at (719) 852-5941, 1803 West Highway 160, Monte Vista, 81144. For information about camping, hiking, and management policies west of the Continental Divide, contact the Durango Forest Service Office at (970) 247-4875, 701 Camino del Rio, Room 301, Durango, 81301.

Spanning the Continental Divide in the San Juans is the Weminuche Wilderness Area. At over 400,000 acres, the Weminuche is the largest wilderness in Colorado and certainly one of the most spectacular. Excellent backcountry fly fishing is found in many parts of the wilderness. Vehicles, including mountain bikes, are prohibited in wilderness areas, and access is limited to foot or horseback. Because help is often a long way away, anglers who visit the wilderness should enter prepared to take care of themselves. Information about the Weminuche Wilderness and the hiking trails that lead along the rivers is available from Rio Grande and San Juan National Forests. Detailed descriptions of the hiking trails that lead into the wilderness and along its rivers can be found in Dennis Gebhardt's self-published *A Backpacking Guide to the Weminuche Wilderness*.

Stretches of the Rio Grande and several smaller streams are managed as state wildlife areas by the Colorado Department of Wildlife. Special regulations apply to the use of this public land, which is often limited to angling. Also along the Rio Grande below South Fork, CDOW has several leases from private landowners to allow anglers access to the river. Current lease information is displayed at access points to the river. See Chapter 5 for details.

Many miles of fine fly-fishing water are held by the Southern Ute tribe. Special permits are required to fish these waters. For details, see Chapter 2.

Something for Everyone

In this book we offer an overview of the fly-fishing opportunities in southern Colorado on both sides of the Continental Divide. More than just a brief outlook for each river or lake is provided—you will find enough in-depth information to visit any reach of a stream and know just what to expect. Select a spot that strikes your fancy and you will be able to show up with the proper rod, line, leader, waders, flies, and expectations.

Each chapter has the details visitors can use to make their first fly-fishing trip to southern Colorado a success. We believe that even readers who are familiar with the San Juans will find some places or techniques here that they haven't tried before.

Southern Colorado offers challenging waters to beginners, intermediates, and experienced fly fishers. However, not all the rivers or lakes are for every angler. Tight, brushy streams, wide-open rivers, slow-moving currents, and roaring creeks are all a part of southern Colorado angling.

Beginners should look for streams or lakes with open banks that are free of vegetation. Streams wider than 15 or 20 feet will provide the easiest casting from just off the bank. Currents should not be too fast or too slow. Good summer-time streams for those just starting in fly fishing are Williams Creek or the East Fork of the San Juan. Beginners looking to hone their skills should avoid the high water of runoff in the spring and the low-flow conditions of fall and concentrate on angling during July and August.

The pocket water, mountain freestone streams, and tail-waters of southern Colorado will challenge intermediate an-glers to improve their techniques. Skills required on such waters include reach and slack-line casts, getting a drag-free float in complex currents, and prospecting for trout in rocky streams. Mountain trout are often forgiving, and the streams of the San Juans are ideal for perfecting these skills. In mid-summer, intermediate anglers will do well to try places like the Rio Grande or te Piedra River.

For experienced anglers, the rivers and creeks of the San Juans offer limitless possibilities in a wide variety of settings. The stillwater bends of Elk Creek will test every angler's pre-sentaion skills. The tight quarters and fast-moving currents of the West Fork of the San Juan make every angling moment there a challenge. Simply working through the brush of the lower Florida River is an adventure for the hardiest fly fishers. Fall angling under low flows on any river can try one's patience and persistence. If you so choose, you don't have to look far to find an angling challenge in the San Juans.

It is our hope you will discover that not every spot in which it is possible to cast a fly on the waters of southern Colorado has been covered in this book. We've kept a couple secrets to ourselves, have not mentioned a few sensitive areas that wouldn't stand an increase in angling pressure, and have left out other water simply because of the amount of fine small-stream angling the region offers. Use this book not as your sole source of information but as a starting point for your own investigations into the streams and lakes of the San Juans.

This book is meant to be a true field guide, so throw it into your truck, stuff it in your backpack, carry it in your back pocket, drop it in a river, spill coffee on it. Read it and use it where it was written, in the heart of the San Juans.

Fishing Localities in Southern Colorado

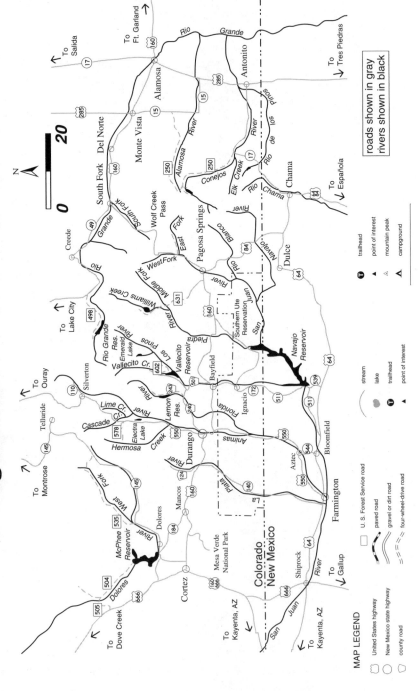

roads shown in gray
rivers shown in black

MAP LEGEND

2

COLORADO FISHING REGULATIONS AND PERSONAL CONSERVATION ETHICS

Colorado's angling season is open all year. Anglers over the age of sixteen must have a valid Colorado fishing license in their possession while they are engaged in the act of angling. Those under the age of sixteen may fish without a license but can take only one-half of the legal limit in any location; however, they may purchase a license and be entitled to a full possession limit.

Under the current statewide system, outdoor recreationists are issued a Colorado Conservation Certificate by vendors for the Colorado Division of Wildlife. License stamps for hunting, trapping, or fishing are purchased to attach to the certificate. The stamps validate the certificate for a specific time period and a specific activity. Anglers must purchase a fishing license stamp. Each year new stamps are attached to the certificate on top of old ones. Hold on to your Conservation Certificate and bring it back the next year when you go to get your new license.

Fees for an annual fishing license stamp are $20.25 for Colorado residents and $40.25 for nonresidents. (The twenty-five cents is a fee that funds backcountry search-and-rescue operations for hunters and fishermen only.) Colorado resident seniors can receive an annual license for $10.25. Short-term licenses are also available. For both residents and nonresidents a one-day stamp is $5.25, a five-day stamp is $18.25.

General bag and possession limits apply in waters that have no special regulations. The bag limit is the number of fish you have in your creel. The possession limit is the maximum number of trout a licensed angler can have in his or her possession at any one time. "In possession" is defined to include the fish you have in a creel, in an ice cooler, in your car, or at home in the freezer. The bag limit and the possession limit are equal. For trout, the possession limit is eight fish of all species combined. The exception to this rule is brook trout: Anglers may possess up to ten brook trout that are 8 inches or less.

License stamp fees, special regulation waters, and bag limits are frequently changed. CDOW updates the fishing regulations for the state every five years, and amendments may be made to the regulations as emergencies arise. The latest set of regulations, issued in 1996, will remain in effect until the end of the year 2000. CDOW provides anglers with a pamphlet detailing the latest regulations that is available wherever licenses are sold. It is recommended that you pick up and carefully read a copy of the latest regulations when you purchase your license stamp.

Special Regulations

In waters with threatened or sensitive populations of trout, special regulations may be in effect. Information on special waters is available in the current regulations pamphlet from CDOW. You can also find information on streams and lakes managed with special regulations in various chapters in this book.

Special regulations usually apply to one or more species of trout found in a stream or lake. The regulations are designed to insure high-quality angling opportunity for the long run and to increase angler satisfaction by increasing the number of large trout found in a stream or lake. The most common regulations are reduced bag limits and size restrictions on the fish that may be kept. We recommend that anglers go a step further in special-regulations areas and restrict angling to the use of artificial flies and lures with single barbless hooks.

In some cases it is deemed necessary for anglers to release all fish back to the water. Within southern Colorado, waters such as the East Fork of Hermosa Creek and the Dolores River below McPhee Dam are managed in such a manner. Catch-and-release angling on the East Fork helps protect a recently reestablished population of native Colorado River cutthroats; the variable nature of flows below the dam necessitates special regulations to the Dolores to protect all species of trout found there.

Colorado Department of Wildlife has two distinct designations for classes of water. Wild Trout Waters hold populations of wild fish, and these waters are no longer stocked. Wild populations include native Colorado River and Rio Grande cutthroats, rainbow trout, and brown trout. Wild trout reproduce naturally in the stream and can be sensitive to angling pressure. These trout are raised in the stream and tend to be more challenging to catch. Many anglers treasure the task of taking a wild trout on a fly. To protect these valuable fish, we encourage all anglers to treat Wild Trout Waters as catch-and-release areas and return all fish to the water.

Gold Medal Waters are assigned sparingly to protect places where anglers may find a trophy fish. Rivers and lakes with this designation are optimum habitat for growing big trout. In southern Colorado, only the Rio Grande between South Fork and Del Norte holds such a distinction.

Southern Ute Reservation Waters

A portion of southern Colorado from south of Pagosa Springs to south of Durango is included in the Southern Ute Indian Reservation. Sections of four important fly-fishing rivers run through the reservation: the San Juan, the Piedra, the Los Pinos, and the Animas. Anglers who wish to visit these waters need to follow the regulations established by the Southern Ute Natural Resources Division.

All anglers on the reservation need to obtain a Southern Ute Non-Member Fishing License from the tribe. Note that a

Colorado Division of Wildlife Wild Trout Waters and other places where popula-tions of wild trout are found, like Lake Creek, should be treated as catch-and-re-lease water. (Photograph by June Fabryka-Martin.)

Colorado license is not required to fish Southern Ute waters. In 1996, two-day permits were $10, five-day were $15, and a season permit was available for $30. Licenses are available from the Southern Ute Natural Resources Division, P.O. Box 737, Ignacio, Colorado 81127, and also at Duranglers at 801B Main Street in Durango. Call the Southern Ute office at (970) 563-0125 if you need additional information. Make certain to pick up the latest copy of the Southern Ute Indian Reservation Fishing Proclamation when you purchase your licence.

Complex land management issues make fishing the Southern Ute waters difficult. Land on the reservation is divided into four major categories. Private land is owned outright and angling without permission of the landowner is prohibited. Other reservation land can be tribal, allotted, or assigned land. Allotted land is tribal land that is leased to a tribal member and is treated as private land: Angling is prohibited except with permission of the allotment holder. Assigned land is treated in the same manner as allotted land. Angling is permitted only on nonallotted and nonassigned tribal land, which is usually, but not always, marked. In all cases, anglers should know exactly what type of tribal land they are on and make certain they have the proper permit and permission before fishing. Study the regulations carefully before heading out to fish the Southern Ute Reservation, and when in doubt, ask.

Private Property

Not all of southern Colorado's attractive fly-fishing streams and lakes are on public land. Many stretches of river flow through private land. In this book we have concentrated on public waters and water on the Southern Ute Reservation where a special-use permit will allow you to fish on open tribal land. We point out private land where it occurs and remind anglers to stay off private property unless permission has been granted.

Unlike some states in the West, in Colorado the bed of a stream flowing through private land is considered private property and is off-limits to anglers. Most private land is well posted, but it is the responsibility of the angler to know the ownership status of a stream before entering to fish it. Staying off private land helps maintain a positive attitude of landowners toward fishermen.

Not all private land is clearly marked with No Trespassing signs. Some landowners post signs declaring Fishing by Permission Only. In this case, anglers are welcome to seek out the owner and ask for permission to fish the stream. When granted such permission, anglers should be especially careful to observe the requests of the owner. Respect the property by leaving no sign of your passage: Use the land only for fishing, close all gates, take out your trash, and consider releasing all fish you catch. Courtesy toward the landowner will help secure permission for the next angler who wishes to use the water.

Self-Regulation

Over the last few years we have witnessed an unprecedented increase in the number of fly fishermen on our waters. Once uncrowded spots on some of our rivers are almost overrun with vested anglers with long rods. Some blame it on "that movie," but the trend began well before Norman Maclean became a well-known author and a film was based on his writing.

The sport of fly fishing offers anglers many reasons to venture forth in all kinds of weather to stand in raging currents and cast a creation of feathers and fur onto the water. Some fishermen are out for meat, looking to put food on their tables in a manner akin to our past. Others are attracted to the water because Brad Pitt looked so smooth wrestling those five-pound brown trout from the Gallatin River. For an increasing number of anglers, fly fishing has less to do with catching trout than with immersing themselves in the trout's world. Fly fishing is often an excuse simply to spend time alone amid the calming scenery of the mountains.

Every angler should ask himself why he wants to catch fish. If the answer is for food, or to achieve an image, then perhaps a message here in support of conservation will do no good. Regardless of motive, every angler has a responsibility to the future. The best way to help insure the survival of trout populations, especially wild and native ones, is to go beyond state-mandated restrictions and practice self-regulation. More and more fishermen find that the regulations of state management agencies do not meet their personal aims. These anglers take the opportunity afforded by the nature of fly fishing to release all or the majority of trout they catch.

In waters without special regulations, the decision to take a trout home or to camp belongs to the skilled individual who brings a trout to the net. If, as is increasingly the case, fly fishing is viewed as recreation and not hunting, is it necessary to kill fish? The value of a day on the stream should be measured in terms of relaxation, self-evaluation, and rejuvenation, not by the number of dead fish in a creel.

At a minimum, meat fishermen should learn to distinguish a wild trout from hatchery fish. To protect wild trout, those out to keep their catch should concentrate their efforts on hatchery fish. Stay near the road and away from naturally reproducing populations. Consider releasing all brown trout and native Colorado River and Rio Grande cutthroats back to the water. Even a large brook trout, a fish who will supply copious quantities of eggs for the next generation of wild fish, should be released.

Anglers who fish for more intangible reasons need not live by a strict no-kill policy. Most trout fishermen would not deny they find a deep satisfaction in eating a part of the catch, especially fresh trout grilled over the campfire. Instead, evaluate each individual catch and determine its effect on the future of trout fishing in the water you fish. Please consider that you can limit your kill; you do not have to kill your limit. We call this self-regulation.

Self-regulation has a few simple goals. Most important is to protect trout species that are threatened or endangered, whether they are officially designated so or not. Rio Grande and Colorado River cutthroats are examples of trout with shrinking populations that require protection. The delicate balance experienced by native cutthroat populations demands that anglers release all native trout.

Self-regulation serves to insure the continuation of quality angling in quality water. Harvesting the larger fish in a trophy trout water only leads to the decline of the size and numbers of the fish caught there. A full-grown trout must be released so that other anglers may have the opportunity to catch it and so that it may live to produce the next generation. This is especially true for trout in wild trout waters. Most anglers agree that self-sustaining populations provide more challenging fishing in a higher quality resource. With no source of new fish other than natural reproduction, these streams should be treated as no-kill areas. Self-regulation reduces the need for stocking of inferior nonwild fish.

If you plan to keep some of your fish, carefully consider each fishing situation on an individual basis. Think of the future of the stream before deciding to kill a trout. Consider the following general guidelines: Release all Colorado River and Rio Grande cutthroats. Carefully return all big fish to the water. Release large brown, rainbow, cutthroat, and brook trout in wild trout waters. Limit your kill to stocked fish.

How to Catch and Release

Simply removing a hook and throwing a trout back into the current will not guarantee that a healthy trout has been returned to the water. After the struggle of fighting against an angler trying to land him, a trout is exhausted. A weakened fish must be properly revived before release: A carelessly handled fish may swim quickly out of sight only to lose its equilibrium, roll over, and float away to die.

Properly releasing a fish begins with a barbless hook. Barbless hooks make it easier to release fish unharmed, and the smaller wedge created by the smashed barb results in more hooked fish. As an added advantage, it is easier to remove a barbless hook accidentally cast into clothing or skin. Some fly shops concerned with maintaining quality fisheries sell flies without barbs, or you can simply flatten the barb with a pair of pliers before casting. Fly tiers can flatten the barb before tying a fly so that if the hook point breaks off they have not wasted time tying the fly.

On the stream, it is important to land a hooked fish as quickly as possible. Do not force a fish in before the fight is truly over; it is better that the fish fight on the end of the line rather than risk injury by wriggling out of your hands and flopping on the ground. Limit the use of a net to larger fish, and be careful not to entangle the fish in the mesh.

After landing a fish, try to keep it in the water. To reduce damage to the mucous layer that protects a fish from infection and disease, never handle a fish with dry hands. Never put your fingers into the gills of a fish. Taking care not to squeeze the fish, hold it with one hand and slip the hook out with the other.

For deeply hooked fish, use needle-nose pliers or hemostats to dislodge the hook. Grasp the hook with the tool, push it back toward the tail, turning it at the same time. If this fails to loosen the hook, cut the leader and leave the fly in the fish. Trout have a natural mechanism for dissolving the hook at the point of contact, and it will be gone in a few days.

Tired fish must be revived before they are released. In calm water, hold the fish so it faces upstream. With one hand, hold the fish by the tail, and use the other hand to support its body from underneath. Gently move the fish back and forth so that oxygen-carrying water flows over the gills. Don't let the fish swim away the first time it tries—often it will swim out of sight only to lose its equilibrium and die. Make sure the fish seems strong enough to hold its own in a quiet current. After a lengthy fight it may take a half an hour to properly revive a fish, but it usually requires one to five minutes. A good rule of thumb is to revive a fish for at least as long as it took to land it.

3

SAFETY AND COMFORT:

Elevation, Weather, and Wildlife of the Southern Colorado Mountains

Weather conditions in the mountains are not to be taken lightly. Temperatures decrease by about five degrees for every 1,000 feet of ascent. By the time you reach 10,000 feet it is always cool—just a breath away from turning cold. Combined with wet conditions, cool temperatures can be deadly. Anyone who spends time in the high country, and particularly fishermen who thrive near water, need to be constantly vigilant concerning the weather. Wet, cold, and wind can quickly lead to hypothermia, a deadly condition brought about when the body's core temperature drops.

Mountain Weather Patterns

The most hazardous characteristic of mountain weather is its quick changes. In the mountains, rapid storm development is the rule rather than the exception. A summer morning can change from lazy sunshine to life-threatening snowstorm in a matter of minutes. Even when the trout have absorbed your total concentration, it is imperative to always keep one eye on the weather.

Preparation is the best way to protect yourself from the vagaries of the weather. Always travel in the mountains prepared for severe weather conditions. No matter how short the journey, carry a raincoat and a change of warm clothing. Stuff a backpack with a lightweight fleece jacket, weatherproof pants, and a waterproof shell.

Another life-threatening weather phenomenon is thunderstorms. Daily heating in southern Colorado's valleys produces rapid-growing cumulonimbus clouds above the peaks. Storms generally begin developing around 10 A.M. and are in full swing by noon. Storms may last throughout the afternoon with periods of heavy rainfall and frequent lightning. Anglers should never venture out even on the sunniest summer mornings without good raingear.

Across the nation, lightning causes about one hundred deaths per year, mostly outdoor recreationists. In southern Colorado, thunderstorms occur fifty to seventy days per year. Anglers, particularly those standing in rivers or on lakeshores, are often the tallest objects in an area. To add slightly to the danger, they hold lightning rods in their hands in the form of their fishing rods. This is true for wet fiberglass rods as well as for graphite ones. Being in a canyon offers some protection but is no guarantee of safety. Anglers are also at risk from ground currents, which are set up when current flows through the ground toward the strike to restore the electrical balance. Ground currents cover a much larger area than the direct hit does, affecting perhaps as much as one hundred feet in all directions from the strike. These high currents are as deadly as the bolt itself. Anglers especially need to be careful: Water is a good conductor of electricity, and ground currents can reach a wading angler through the water.

Anglers seldom seek shelter from a storm until they start to get wet. However, lightning can occur several miles in front of or behind a storm. Lightning-caused deaths most often occur at the beginning or end of a storm, when no rain is falling.

When a thunderstorm rolls in, the safest place to be is in your car. If reaching shelter is impossible, minimize the lightning danger by avoiding ridges, peaks, and open meadows. Get out of and away from the water, and avoid lone trees or rocks. Stay out of depressions, shallow caves, and overhangs, all places where ground currents can jump across the openings. Good protection is afforded by groups of same-sized trees. If you are caught in the open, lay your rod flat on the ground and get at least thirty feet away from it. Crouch down (don't lie flat), place your feet close together, and put your hands on your knees. This will minimize the chance of ground currents using your body as a path for electrons.

Dressing for Comfort

Dressing comfortably in mountain climates can pose a challenge. The thin atmosphere at high elevations holds less heat, permitting wild daily temperature fluctuations. Days can be uncomfortably hot, then temperatures can plummet below freezing at night.

Spring weather is characterized by cool days and cold nights. Even in the lower elevations, temperatures in the day can stay below 55 degrees and at night can dip into the teens. The wind is a constant factor in spring. Fast-moving cold fronts can turn a sunny afternoon into a blizzard in a couple of hours. The secret to springtime comfort is warm clothing and a solid windbreaker. Carry a second jacket for the late afternoon, when temperatures drop. Always carry a waterproof shell in case of a sudden snowstorm.

In summer, daytime highs average in the lower eighties, but may reach the nineties in lower elevations. In the high terrain, temperatures rarely leave the seventies. At night, ice may form in the coffeepot along high lakes, and temperatures in the forties are the rule in the lower elevations. Rain showers are common in the afternoons, but storms seldom last all day. However, be watchful for tropical moisture streaming into the mountains from the southwest in late summer. Such storms can dump several inches of precipitation over two or three rainy days and turn a dream fishing trip into a soggy nightmare.

To stay comfortable in summer, layer your clothes. Shorts are acceptable on sunny days, but carry fleece pants in case the weather turns bad and for the evening. Light cotton shirts can be layered with fleece jackets for most conditions, but when the weather turns wet, polypropylene shirts protect against the cold. Fleece jackets make warm evening wear. Again, always carry a waterproof jacket and rain pants.

Fall can bring some of the year's most delightful weather to the mountains, and the scenery is enhanced by golden aspens on the slopes. In September and early October one can count on sunny days and cool nights. Jackets will be appreciated in morning and evening, and warmer wear is necessary at night. Synthetic shirts are well suited for a base layer, with fleece on top.

Although fall can be pleasant, it is not unusual for a September snowstorm to blow in and shut the mountains down for a day or two. Anglers planning a fall trip to the San Juans should have a recent weather forecast in hand. If a cold front is headed your way, consider postponing the trip for a couple of days. Rest assured that brilliant sunshine will return.

Elevation Factors

At 6,800 feet, Colorado has the highest average elevation of all fifty states. Elevations in southern Colorado range from 6,100 feet where the Animas River exits the state to 14,309 feet on Uncompahgre Peak, the highest point in the San Juans. Durango sits at 6,500 feet and Silverton at 9,300 feet. The access points to most streams lie in the range of 6,500 to 9,000 feet, climbing to headwaters at around 12,000 feet.

The high elevations of the fishing waters of southern Colorado have important consequences for fly fishermen. The concentration of oxygen in the air decreases with increasing elevation. At 9,000 feet, only half the oxygen available at sea level is in the atmosphere. Above 5,000 feet, anyone coming from sea level will notice the difference. A stroll down the streets of Durango can induce some labored breathing; climbing a talus slope along a mountain lake at 11,000 feet can be totally exhausting.

At over 9,000 feet, even the short walk from River Hill into the head of Box Canyon on the Rio Grande can be taxing for those unaccustomed to high altitudes. (Photograph by Craig Martin.)

All anglers need to be aware of the need to slow down at high elevations. All actions will require more exertion. Anglers coming from lower elevations should be prepared to take it easy when hiking to and wading in streams. The best advice is to spend several days at intermediate elevations before venturing above 8,000 feet. When you first arrive in the mountains, plan on fishing streams or lakes in the 5,000- to 7,000-foot range before heading to the high country.

Anglers heading above 9,000 feet should be aware of a potentially serious medical condition called *mountain sickness*. The condition is induced by a rapid ascent to high altitudes. Symptoms include headache, nausea, muscle weakness, and shortness of breath, with symptoms generally worse in the morning. A gradual ascent to elevations over

9,000 feet will usually prevent illness. If you show signs of mountain sickness, dropping back to a lower elevation will usually improve your condition. If the symptoms persist, seek medical assistance.

Sunshine and Altitude

Brilliant sunny days in the high country pose a special kind of danger to those who come unprepared. It is no accident that skin cancer rates from overexposure to the sun are high in the Southwest. The thin atmosphere and low humidity block very little of the sun's ultraviolet radiation, and anglers must provide their own protection from the sun.

Before each fishing trip, start with a heavy coat of sunscreen with at least an SPF 15 rating. Coat all areas of exposed skin: hands, arms, face, and the back of the neck. Wearing a long-sleeved shirt will offer greater protection. Wear a sturdy wide-brimmed hat. Protect your eyes with a pair of polarized sunglasses that are rated to block at least 95 per cent of both UVA and UVB radiation.

Water and Dehydration

Plentiful sunshine, low humidity, and exertion combine to readily dehydrate anglers. Drying of body tissue can lead to anything from a simple headache to a severe condition requiring medical attention. When you feel thirsty, chances are your body is already a quart low on fluids. A headache at the end of a day may be a sign of dehydration. Thus, anglers should consider making it a point to drink at least a half-gallon of water every day they spend in the high country. Water from streams and lakes is probably contaminated with *Giardia* and should not be used without treatment by boiling, filtering, or by chemical means. Carry water with you on short fishing excursions, and plan to treat water on extended stays in the backcountry.

Critters

Ticks are common in grasses in mountain meadows, particularly in spring and early summer. Two potentially serious illnesses can result from tick bites. Rocky Mountain spotted fever is a flulike disease with symptoms of high fever, muscle aches, and a red rash. Medical attention is required. Colorado tick fever is similar but is less severe. Lyme disease is thus far absent from southern Colorado but may soon appear here.

In any case, make a careful inspection for ticks following all fishing trips. If you find an embedded tick, don't attempt to pull it out but rather drive it out with a match that has been struck and extinguished or a dab of alcohol on a cloth. Those who find embedded ticks should be observant for symptoms of serious illness for several weeks.

Rattlesnakes are uncommon above 7,000 feet, but anglers along the lower Animas, Dolores, Piedra, Rio Grande, and Conejos Rivers should be watchful for snakes. These snakes are easily avoided by keeping hands and feet out of uninspected places whenever walking through rocks and brush.

4

THE CONEJOS WATERSHED

CONEJOS RIVER

Managed by: Rio Grande National Forest, South San Juan
Wilderness Area, private
Access by: Vehicle and foot
Altitude: 7,200 to 12,100 feet
Type of Water: Freestone stream, riffle and pool, pocket
water, meadow-lined headwaters
Best Times: Early July to mid-October
Hatches: Salmon flies, abundant mayflies, brown drakes,
caddisflies
Maps: Rio Grande National Forest; USGS Summit Peak, Pla-
toro, Red Mountain, Spectacle Lake, La Jara Canyon,
and Osier 7.5' quadrangles

The Conejos (*cone-AY-hos*) River flows 70 miles from the
Continental Divide in the San Juan Mountains across the San
Luis Valley to meet the Rio Grande. Along the way, the Conejos passes through high meadows, rugged canyons, and the
lush bottomlands of a broad glacial valley carved in volcanic
rocks. The river's long course through this variety of terrain
creates a diversity of fly-fishing opportunity rarely found on a

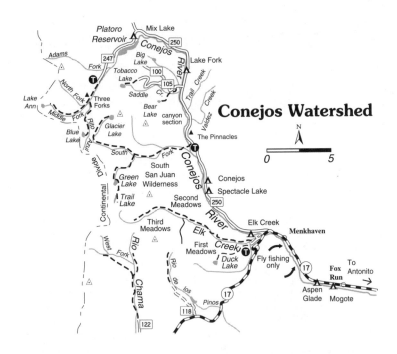

single river. Broad meanders on the flat valley floor of the lower and middle Conejos are well suited to the dry-fly fisherman, the upper headwaters provide walk-in water for the small stream enthusiast, and the churning pocket water of the rugged canyon provides those willing to make the rough trip ample opportunity to fish for wild browns and rainbows with nymphs and streamers. Best of all, access to every type of angling, even in high meadows at 10,000 feet, is relatively easy.

The headwaters of the Conejos, which means "rabbits" in Spanish, flow from the South San Juan Wilderness Area. The main river is formed from three small branches that plunge from the forest below the highest peaks to flow through small meadow-lined glacial valleys and meet in the area called Three Forks. Below the high meadows the river is impounded into Platoro Reservoir, one of the highest man-made lakes in North America. Several miles of meadow water with deep undercut banks are found below Platoro, then the river dives into two steep-walled canyons. Huge boulders that fell into the stream from the cliffs above create deep pockets, churning currents, and fine trout habitat. Indeed, this stretch is the best on the river.

Exiting the canyons at the confluence with the South Fork of the Conejos, the river flows for many miles through a wide valley carved by glaciers. Much of the water in this stretch is controlled by private owners, but a short stretch near Spectacle Lake and Conejos Campgrounds offers good fishing. Below Colorado 17, the Conejos continues to flow peacefully with sweeping turns on the valley floor through a mixture of public and private land. Near Menkhaven, a 4-mile stretch of fly-fishing-only water offers public access to large pools and long riffles. More public water is found surrounding Aspen Glade and Mogote Campgrounds. From the village of Fox Run the river flows on private land to meet the Rio Grande on the flats of the San Luis Valley.

The Conejos is located in the eastern San Juans just west of Antonito. From U.S. 285, which runs south from Salida and Alamosa and north from Santa Fe, head west on Colorado 17 about 15 miles to Aspen Glade Campground. From here, Colorado 17 parallels the lower Conejos and offers easy access to the riffle-and-pool stretch around the campground and the fly-fishing-only water near Menkhaven. About 23 miles from Antonito the river turns north and is paralleled by Forest Road 250 all the way to Platoro Reservoir. This dirt road can be driven by any vehicle, but stretches turn into mud and become impassable for short periods during the summer rainy season. Note that Forest Road 250 can also be reached via Colorado–New Mexico 17 25 miles north of Chama, New Mexico.

Antonito offers gas, basic supplies, and economical lodging. Those seeking fancy accommodations, restaurants, or supermarkets will need to use Alamosa, 60 miles from the river, as a base. Six Forest Service campgrounds are located along the Conejos from Mogote on the lower river near Fox Run to

Mix Lake at Platoro Reservoir. The campgrounds fill quickly during July and August, so plan on arriving early in the day on summer weekends.

The headwater forks of the Conejos are small, averaging six to ten feet in width. Below Platoro Reservoir the Conejos ranges from twenty to sixty feet in width, with the deepest pools about ten feet. The freestone water around Three Forks has a bottom of clean gravel, as do the meadows below Platoro. Wading is easy in these stretches, and in summer wet wading or hip boots are ideal. From the canyons below Platoro downstream the river bottom is composed of cobbles and boulders. The uneven bottom contains deep holes and the currents can be strong. Caution is required for wading in these areas, and chest waders with a wading belt are necessary. Currents moderate in the stretch of water parallel to Colorado 17, but deep holes are common and caution is advised when wading there. The prevalence of surrounding private land and the rocky canyons make floating this small river impossible.

Beginning fly fishermen will find the Conejos a delight on several accounts, not the least of which is the ease of casting on the entire river. The meadow water above and below Platoro offers banks free of leader-snagging vegetation. The rest of the river is wide enough to provide easy casting from within the stream in spite of the willows that often line the banks. In the lower glacial valley below the canyons the stream is lined with cottonwoods or conifers that shade much of the river in the late afternoon.

Anglers will find almost any length rod is appropriate to make casts on the Conejos. Short lightweight rods are ideal in the headwaters, where fish are small and the casting requirements are undemanding. These rods can also be used on calm days in the meadow section. For the canyon reach, 8½ to 9-foot rods are needed to power casts to difficult-to-reach places in the pocket water. Required casting distances expand on the lower river, where long rods are the best bet. Big fish are found throughout the river, and anglers would do well to come

The headwaters of the Conejos River are as scenic a place to cast a fly as you will find anywhere in Colorado. (Photograph by Craig Martin.)

prepared with heavy tippets from 2X to 5X. Conejos browns can run into backing, so make certain all of your tackle is ready for work.

Brown and rainbow trout are found in the Conejos below Platoro, with brook trout added to the mix above the reservoir. Native Rio Grande cutthroats swim the waters of the Lake Fork, a small tributary to the upper river. Rainbows are stocked in many stretches of the river, but the fly-fishing-only stretch near Menkhaven is managed as Wild Trout Water. Around Three Forks, fish average 8 to 10 inches, with an occasional larger brown found in deep water. Below Platoro, trout range from 10 to 22 inches, with most in the 12-inch class. Large rainbows and browns can be found in the deep pools of the canyons, behind rocks in the glacial valley, and in the long riffles of the lower stretch. Plenty of fish are found throughout the river.

Several stretches of the Conejos have special regulations. The fly-fishing-only water near Menkhaven has a two-fish bag and possession limit, and the trout must be 16 inches or longer. From Saddle Creek downstream to the South Fork of the Conejos angling is limited to flies and lures only, and the bag and possession limit is two fish over 16 inches. Also, Lake Fork of the Conejos from the headwaters to Rock Lake is fly-and-lure-only water, and catch-and-release for all cutthroats.

Supporting the large biomass of trout are large populations of aquatic insects. Caddisflies are abundant on all stretches of the river, and common adult and larval caddis patterns such as the Elk Hair Caddis, Green Caddis Larva, and soft-hackles are effective everywhere. Most caddis range from size 10 to 16, and they come in tan, brown, and olive. Both large and small stoneflies are found in the river. Salmon flies and other large stoneflies occur and make fishing large stonefly nymphs effective anywhere on the Conejos below Platoro. Other common nymph patterns that work well on the river are the Hare's Ear, Prince Nymph, and Pheasant Tail, both traditional and beadhead, in sizes 8–14.

Mayfly hatches create exciting dry-fly fishing on the entire river. Swarms of these insects cloud the evening sky throughout early summer. Of particular importance is a large brown drake that comes off the water from mid-June to early July. Following years of normal or high snowpack, this hatch coincides with the later stages of runoff, making wading and dry-fly fishing difficult. With clear water, which usually comes around the second week in July, the trout eagerly take these insects, and fishing with a size 10 or 12 Brown or Gray Wulff can produce a memorable evening of excitement. Other mayflies hatch throughout the season, including a red quill in late June to mid-July, pale morning duns in late July, pale evening duns in August, and blue-winged olives in the fall.

When fishing these fine hatches seek out rising fish, which will be more plentiful in late morning and the evening. Cast to spotted fish, floating your imitation with as little drag as possible. Use a hatch-matching pattern as an attractor and cast it to prime lies such as pockets between boulders or undercuts with converging currents.

Attractor patterns work well from mid-July until fall. Try an Adams, Rio Grande Trude, Royal Wulff, Humpy, or Elk Hair Caddis in sizes 12 to 16. Hopper and ant patterns are perfect in the meadows during August and September, particularly on windy afternoons. High-floating attractors are necessary in the choppy pocket water of the canyons throughout the season. Here flotation and presentation far outweigh the importance of pattern selection, so try the classic western patterns such as any of the Wulffs, Humpy, House and Lot, Irresistible, and Elk Hair Caddis. In the deep pools of the canyons, quick-sinking nymphs and streamers are required. Use size 8–12 beadhead nymphs, weighted stonefly patterns, and large Woolly Buggers.

Unreliable access and cold water temperatures make spring fishing on the Conejos difficult. Runoff begins in mid- to late April and, depending on winter snowpack, continues through mid-June to mid-July. The river generally remains clear during runoff, but strong currents make wading dangerous and dragfree drifts impossible. Following winters with low snowfall in the high country the river may be fishable by the third week in June, but most years conditions are favorable by the Fourth of July. The river remains in prime condition through the summer, though hot weather can slow the action during early and mid-August.

The Conejos Valley takes on a special magic in the fall, a favorite time of year for many Conejos anglers. Yellowing cottonwoods line the river, in sharp contrast to conifer-covered valley walls. The trout remain active through October, especially on warm, sunny afternoons. Fish with general attractors, particularly caddis imitations like the Elk Hair Caddis. Hoppers can be effective as long as the weather stays warm.

With at least 40 miles of public water from which to choose, the Conejos presents anglers with a joyful dilemma:

Where to fish? For scenery, easy fishing, and solitude, it is hard to beat the river and forks above Platoro. A short day hike or backpack will take anglers into the heart of the area at Three Forks where fishing is fine in all directions. The North Fork, Middle Fork, and El Rito Azul are reached via a two-mile hike from the end of the road above Platoro Reservoir. Trails lead up each of the forks, with the Middle Fork offering the best fly fishing for small trout

Those interested in less driving and walking can find fine stretches of public water surrounding Lake Fork and Spectacle Lake Campgrounds. More fine water is found from Aspen Glade Campground upstream about 4 miles to Menkhaven. Each of these reaches offers roadside access, thick summer insect hatches, and huge in-stream boulders that protect goodsized trout.

Near the jagged rock spires of the Pinnacles, the canyon section of the Conejos has the most to offer the adventurous angler. The canyon is rough, rugged, and far from the road. Deep holes and dangerous currents require caution, but the solitude and the wild trout make the trip worthwhile. This stretch of the river is fly-and-lure only, and two fish over 16 inches is the limit.

For the easiest access, park at the trailhead for the South Fork Trail on Forest Road 250, about 15 miles from Colorado 17. The trail leads to the river and crosses it on a footbridge. Walk upstream on the river at least a quarter-mile before casting. More difficult access is found along Valdez and Trail Creeks. Follow the drainages into the gorge, dropping about six hundred feet to the river from the road. These challenging routes are located about 2 and 3 miles above the South Fork Trailhead parking area. Once you are at the river, it is unlikely that anyone will disrupt your solitude.

Long riffles and pocket water are found in the depths of the canyon. Wear chest waders to make the deep crossings that are necessary to continue working your way upstream. Cast to the thousands of likely lies along the river: the tails of riffles, deep pools, behind and in front of large in-stream boulders, and in the many pockets. Use high-floating dry flies or nymphs and keep casts short. Deep pools and steep cliffs pinching against the river make it impossible to wade through the entire canyon except during the lowest flows.

The Rocky Mountain Angling Club holds leases on several fine stretches of the Conejos, including the river's inviting big meanders upstream from Colorado 17. This stretch of the river is among the finest, but angling is limited to club members only. For information on membership and access to this private water, contact the Rocky Mountain Angling Club at 1 (800) 524-1814.

ELK CREEK

Managed by: Rio Grande National Forest, South San Juan Wilderness Area
Access by: Vehicle and foot
Altitude: 7,500 to 11,000 feet
Type of Water: Swift pocket water, flat meadow water
Best Times: July to October
Hatches: Stoneflies, pale morning duns
Maps: Rio Grande National Forest; USGS Spectacle Lake and Victoria Lake 7.5' quadrangles

Anglers visiting the Conejos Watershed in search of a challenging fishing experience should take a stroll up Elk Creek. This major tributary of the Conejos heads in a 10-mile glacial valley against the Continental Divide and alternates between meandering across flat meadows and diving through boulder-strewn canyons. The turbulent waters of the canyons and the glassy still water of the meadows provide contrasting challenges to the angler. No matter where you choose to go, fishing Elk

Creek is never dull. Conditions can be excellent all summer, from the end of runoff in late June to late September.

Access to Elk Creek by road is limited to two places: Elk Creek Campground and the nearby La Manga Trailhead. Both are located on the entrance road just off Colorado 17. A quarter mile past the intersection with Forest Road 250, which is about 23 miles west of Antonito, bear right onto a gravel road marked for Elk Creek Campground. Bear right again to reach the campground. Elk Creek runs through the site, where fishing is fair for stocked rainbows. To reach the La Manga Trailhead, continue straight past the campground entrance road and arrive at the trailhead in one mile. From the large parking area a trail begins downhill and across the bridge over Elk Creek. The Elk Creek Trail parallels the creek for 12 miles, providing access to the entire stream. Climbing about 2,000 feet over those miles, the trail is of moderate difficulty.

Immediately above the La Manga Trailhead Elk Creek is composed of swift pocket water dropping through a narrow canyon with steep slopes. The trail stays above the stream, offering occasional access when the two are squeezed together by the cliffs. At times it is an easy descent to the stream, but more often it is a steep drop to reach the water. Use caution on the steep slopes, where losing one's balance or turning an ankle are real possibilities.

Cascades, plunge pools, choppy riffles, and a few deep holes characterize this stretch of Elk Creek. The creek ranges from ten to twenty feet in width with a few holes up to six feet deep. The water is usually clear with good visibility down to the bottom of the deepest still pools. The rounded boulders and cobbles on the stream bottom are always slippery.

This is no place for beginning fly fishermen. Heavy vegetation along the banks makes casting difficult and often impossible, and the fast currents make wading dangerous. Hip boots are useful to keep your feet dry while walking along the banks, and 7- to 8-foot rods work well in these cramped conditions.

Brown, rainbow, and brook trout from 8 to 14 inches are found in the lower stretches of Elk Creek. Above La Manga Trailhead browns predominate through First Meadows, with the fish here ranging from 10 to 16 inches. Larger rainbows and browns are found in and around Second Meadows. Further upstream, cutthroats are mixed with the rainbows and browns, and the fish are smaller. In the headwaters only cutthroats are found.

Abundant stoneflies, particularly golden stoneflies, are found in the fast-moving water, but most currents are so fast that trout have little time to look over potential food. For the fly fisherman this means pattern selection is not critical. Any high-floating dry fly or large nymph pattern can be effective. Hair-bodied flies, like the Humpy or Irresistible, or heavy-hackled Wulffs in brown, gray, or Royal, are the best bet for drys. Use plenty of floatant on your flies and leader.

Trout will hold in any area of reduced current and anglers should work slowly upstream, using short casts to pop a fly into any slack water amid the rocks. Try along the bank, in pockets, in the current seams behind boulders, in the cushion of water in front of rocks, at the heads of plunge pools, and in the few places the water runs over a foot deep. Short casts will help reduce drag, and use lots of rod manipulation to keep line off the water. In fast water such as this it takes only one or two seconds of good float to induce a strike.

Drifting nymphs through the riffles and pockets is another good technique for Elk Creek. Use weighted patterns that sink quickly in the currents. Hare's Ears, Pheasant Tails, and any variation of the stonefly nymph are perfect choices in the pockets and riffles. As in dry-fly fishing, keep the fly line off the water, using short-line nymphing techniques to search for trout. In the clear, deep pools, streamers are also effective. Try black Woolly Buggers, Little Brown Trout streamers, or stonefly patterns fished deep, perhaps with some weight added to the leader to help the fly sink quickly to the bottom.

About 3 miles up from La Manga Trailhead, Elk Creek reaches First Meadows, one of southern Colorado's most delightful places. The first view of the meadow from the trail is unforgettable: Elk Creek meanders through a flat, open valley with conifer slopes above and a waterfall on the opposite slope. A few campsites are found near the head of the meadow, inviting an overnight stay.

The still waters of the flat valley floor are a complete contrast to the plunging currents below and above, and anglers need a new bag of tricks. Here stealth, fly selection, and careful presentation are important. A quiet, low-profile approach to the stream is required, and accurate, delicate casts are a must. Anglers get only one chance with most of these trout. Light tippets—6X or 7X—will help, as will cross-country casting, where the fly line lands on the banks and only the leader and tippet are on the water. The fishing in the meadows can be superb, particularly in the evening.

Mayfly hatches occur in July, with pale morning and evening duns coming off the meadow water almost all month. For the best results, use size 14 or 16 tan-, gray-, or ginger-bodied flies tied parachute-style, or PMD Comparaduns. In August, hopper patterns are effective from late morning to evening. Dave's Hopper, Schroeder's Parachute Hopper, and Madam X, sizes 10 to 14, are effective in this water. Ant and beetle patterns work well along the banks all day. A splashy cast with a hopper may work, but for other patterns a quiet landing is a must.

Above First Meadows the trail and stream enter another wooded canyon section where fishing conditions are much like those below the meadow. The second canyon is about 2 miles long, ending at Second Meadows 6 miles from the trailhead. Fishing is excellent along the 2-mile length of the meadow. Rumors of large browns and rainbows often come down from Second Meadows, but the long hike in, which requires a backpack trip to be worthwhile, keeps most anglers away. The stillwater meanders of the stream in these meadows require the same careful techniques as in First Meadows, but the trout see fewer anglers here and are not as wary as are those below. The same patterns and techniques that are effective in the meadow below will work here, too. For the larger trout in these waters, use a heavier tippet.

RIO CHAMA

Managed by: Rio Grande National Forest, private
Access by: Foot and mountain bike
Altitude: 8,700 to 10,500 feet
Type of Water: Small freestone stream, meadow water, beaver ponds
Best Times: Mid- to late July to mid-September
Hatches: Small mayflies
Maps: USFS Rio Grande National Forest; USGS Archuleta Creek 7.5' quadrangle

The Rio Chama is a major tributary of the Rio Grande in New Mexico. Its headwaters lie just over the ridge from the headwaters of Elk Creek in the South San Juan Wilderness, giving the upper Chama more affinity with the waters of the Conejos River than with the Rio Grande. The river heads in the Chama Basin, where banded cliffs, grassy ridgelines, and volcanic peaks make a delightful backdrop to angling. Few fishermen are found along the upper river, but when the water runs clear there are plenty of trout eager to try a fly.

The upper Chama is a small freestone stream ranging from fifteen to twenty-five feet wide. The water is never deep, and there are a few holes up to four feet in depth. On the public water upstream from the end of Forest Road 121 the river is brush-lined as it flows through a wide meadow. In places the river runs through braided channels, but mostly it moves over a cobble bottom and around gravel bars. Many two- to three-foot runs along the banks hold fish.

The streamside vegetation makes casting from the bank difficult. It is best to cast from midstream or from the many gravel bars along the river. The water can be cold, but either wet wading or hip boots are appropriate in summer. Rods should be from 7 to 8 feet, with light lines from 3-weight to 5-weight.

Anglers will find mostly wild brown trout in the upper Chama. Rainbows are common, and a few cutbow hybrids are also found here. Most fish are in the 10- to 12-inch range, with a few browns in prime lies reaching up to 18 inches.

Lying away from paved roads, the fish of the upper Chama are spooky, and presentation is always more important than fly selection. Casts should be on target the first time and should land quietly on the water. High-floating flies are best in the riffles and runs along the banks, but parachute and no-hackle patterns are required in the stillwater holes and slower currents. Don't hesitate to put a fly under overhanging vegetation, into a tangle or tree roots, or to fish downstream to hard-to-reach lies. A few lost flies is a small price to pay for landing one of the wild fighters that usually are found in such well-protected locations.

Insects are not abundant in this cold water, but caddisflies are common, and small mayfly hatches throughout the summer are an important food source for the trout. The mayflies include small red quills and *Baetis* species that hatch in the afternoon and evening into mid-September. Terrestrials are important all along the stream, particularly when grasshoppers fill the meadows in August and September. Hopper patterns in the meadows and ants or beetles floated along the banks are often the angler's best bet on the upper Chama.

Unstable volcanic soils in the upper Chama Basin can create serious problems for trout and the angler. Mud slides are common in the basin, and a huge recent slide scar is visible on the east slope of the canyon. Following rapid snowmelt in the spring and heavy rains during the summer months, the mud often reaches the river, turning it into a brown torrent. Turbid conditions can last for days or weeks, rendering the stream unfishable. Thus it is best to avoid the upper Chama during and after periods of heavy precipitation.

One and a half miles above the end of Forest Road 121 the character of the Chama changes as the river passes through a small canyon. The banks are even more brushy, and the stream is shallower as it becomes more like pocket water. Look for trout in runs over a foot deep, under vegetation along the banks, and pop flies into the pockets under trees and behind rocks. About 4 miles above the campground the stream splits into the East and West Forks. In this area, best reached via Trail 738, numerous beaver ponds offer challenging stillwater fishing for 10- to 14-inch browns and cutthroats.

The Rio Chama flows through private land along New Mexico 17 north of Chama, New Mexico. Public water is reached off New Mexico 17 via Forest Road 121, which is located 5 miles north of Chama and 45 miles west of Antonito on Colorado–New Mexico 17. Turn north on Forest Road 121 and continue 6 miles through private land. A primitive campground is located off the road along the river, and Forest Road 121 ends a short distance above the campground. Trail 122 begins across the Chama from the campground. Fording the stream may be difficult before mid-July due to high water. The trail leads north along the Chama from the campground for 2 miles before splitting with Trail 740, heading west along the West Fork of the Rio Chama, and Trail 738, heading north along the East Fork. In a half-mile Trail 738 crosses the Chama and continues another 2 miles to end at an old cabin site near some beaver ponds. Mountain bikes can easily make the trip to the trail fork, and a bit of pushing will take the rider farther up the East Fork. The trail up the West Fork is too steep and easily eroded for bicycles.

Conejos Area Lakes

Of the two dozen or so lakes found in the high country above the Conejos River and its tributaries, about a dozen are fine trout lakes. Although no roads lead to any of the lakes, they are favorite destinations for fly fishermen who don't mind a good walk in the South San Juan Wilderness.

The lakes are similar in character and provide the same basic kind of angling opportunities. They range in size from ten to about one hundred acres, and all are deep enough to protect against winterkill. Elevations range from that of Beaver Lake, at 9,700 feet, to that of Lake Ann, tucked up against the Continental Divide at almost 12,000 feet. All have fine insect populations to support trout, with caddisflies and mayflies, particularly *Callibaetis* species, most important.

The easiest trout lakes to reach are Beaver and Duck, which are part of the Elk Creek drainage. Both lakes are reached via the Duck Lake Trail, beginning at the west side of the La Manga Trailhead 25 miles west of Antonito. (See page 42 for details on access to the trailhead.) The trail is easy to follow, but it has several steep sections while gaining 1,300 feet to Duck Lake. Beaver Lake is about 2 miles up the trail, and the larger Duck Lake is about 3 miles from the trailhead. Both lakes receive moderate pressure from anglers going for brook and cutthroat trout in the 10- to 16-inch range. Midges can be important in these lakes, and midge pupae fished just under the surface can be very effective in the evening.

Two rough dirt roads, Forest Road 105 and Forest Road 100, provide access to the trailheads for three large lakes in the northern Conejos watershed. Forest Road 105 is located about 15 miles on Forest Road 250 from Colorado 17. The road requires a four-wheel-drive and can be hazardous when wet, which is often all summer long. The trip up Forest Road 105 makes a challenging climb on a mountain bike. The Bear Lake Trail begins at a hairpin turn on Forest Road 105 about a mile from Forest Road 250. Bear Lake is 3 miles from and 2,000 feet above the trailhead, a strenuous climb. About 6 miles from Forest Road 250, Forest Road 100 splits off to the right, leading to the trailhead for Big Lake. The trail drops 1,000 feet in a mile to reach the lake, and it is a steep climb back to the road. The Tobacco Lake Trailhead is off Forest Road 105 about 10 miles from Forest Road 250. This high lake is 800 feet above the trailhead and over a mile from the road.

Big Lake supports a population of native cutthroats and brown trout and is managed as catch-and-release water. Fishing is difficult in the clear water. Bear Lake holds brook, rainbow, and brown trout up to 18 inches. Fishing can be good in the morning during mayfly hatches and in the evening on caddis and streamer patterns. Tobacco Lake, sitting at the foot of Conejos Peak, is a typical glacial lake. Cutthroats are found here ranging up to 18 inches, but fish are not as plentiful as in the lower lakes.

Four high-country lakes require considerable effort to reach. Of these, Blue Lake is the easiest to reach but still involves a six-mile hike with a 1,500-foot elevation gain. The lake lies near the Rito Azul Trail about 4 miles from Three Forks above Platoro Reservoir. Park at the trailhead 7 miles above the village of Platoro and hike 2 miles on the Three Forks Trail to the junction with the Rito Azul Trail. Turn left and cross the Conejos, then climb steadily along El Rito Azul to reach the lake. Blue Lake is one of the largest lakes in the Conejos drainage and supports 10- to 20-inch rainbows and cutthroats. Midges and streamers are important patterns for this lake.

Lake Ann is also reached from Three Forks. To get to the lake, continue up the Middle Fork of the Conejos on the well-defined trail that follows the valley. After 4 miles, climb above timberline to cross the Continental Divide Trail and reach the lake about 6 miles from the trailhead. The setting of this 11,900-foot lake is spectacular, and the fishing is good for cutthroats and rainbows up to 15 inches.

Deep in the South San Juan Wilderness are Green and Trail Lakes. Both lakes require long hikes to reach and are best visited as part of an extended stay in the backcountry. They lie on the plateau between the South Fork of the Conejos to the north and Elk Creek to the south. To reach them, hike up the South Fork Trail from the trailhead, which is about 12 miles up Forest Road 250 from Colorado 17. It is twelve miles to Green Lake via the South Fork and Cañon Verde Trails. The latter trail is steep, making a 2,000-foot climb over 4 miles. Trail Lake is about 3 miles farther south on the Continental Divide Trail. Both lakes hold large cutthroats and rainbows that can make the long trip in and out worthwhile. Plan on at least a three-day adventure to fish either or both of these lakes.

5

THE UPPER RIO GRANDE WATERSHED

RIO GRANDE

Managed by: Rio Grande National Forest, Colorado Department of Wildlife, private
Access by: Vehicle and foot
Altitude: 7,200 to 12,400 feet
Type of Water: Wide freestone stream, pocket water, riffles and pools
Best Times: Late June to late September
Hatches: Salmon fly, golden stonefly, caddisflies, green drake, slate-wing dun, other mayflies
Maps: USFS Rio Grande National Forest; USGS Pole Creek Mountain, Finger Mesa, Little Squaw Creek, Bristol Head, Workman Creek, Creede, Wagon Wheel Gap, South Fork West, South Fork East, and Indian Head 7.5' quadrangles

The writers of Western novels, along with Hollywood filmmakers, have painted a lasting but false impression of the river called the Rio Grande. The Spanish words meaning "big river" conjure up an image of dusty weather-beaten cowboys crossing a desert plain to a muddy sheet of water. Indeed, the Rio Grande is such a river in southern New Mexico and Texas,

51

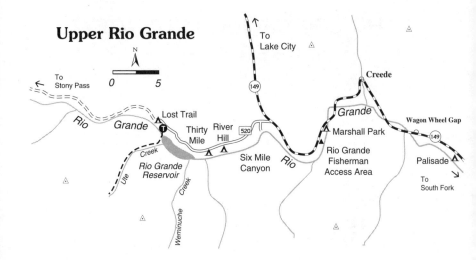

for the last four-fifths of its journey to the Gulf of Mexico. But eighteen hundred miles upstream from salt water the Rio Grande flows through another world, one of snowcapped peaks and aspen-dotted slopes.

The upper watershed of the Rio Grande in the San Juan Mountains provides some of the finest trout fishing in Colorado. In almost all of its reaches the river is a consistent producer of large trout. For sheer pleasure, one can fish the river for a week and enjoy a different type of angling experience every day, from small stream commando fishing to floating a broad river. Not all fishermen come away pleased with the Rio Grande, but skilled and patient anglers will quickly fall under the river's spell.

The Rio Grande, the second longest river in the United States, heads in the high mountains between Creede and Silverton. The river's mountain journey takes it 60 miles east to the San Luis Valley where, near Alamosa, it turns south to flow into New Mexico. From the headwaters to Del Norte, the Rio Grande is fine trout water, including a stretch between South Fork and Del Norte where the slow-moving meandering river is designated Gold Medal Water. Within this westward bulge in the Continental Divide the river is joined by about fifty tributaries, each of which offers classic small-stream angling for small trout. With small creeks, pocket water, wide riffles, and pools, the upper Rio Grande offers the fly fisher anything his or her heart desires.

In the early 1980s much of the upper river held only small rainbows and browns. In 1984, the Colorado Department of Wildlife introduced a strain of wild rainbows from the Colorado River to the upper Rio Grande and enacted special regulations to help the new rainbows and the resident browns stabilize. The upper Rio Grande soon became a blue ribbon fishery. The rainbows are now self-sustaining, but flow patterns and whirling disease have taken their toll, and the population is not as large as it was. The rainbows are hearty, strong, and smart, with a few fish still reaching 18 inches or more. Despite the presence of rainbows, brown trout remain the heart of the fishery, and they are plentiful.

The towns of Del Norte, South Fork, and Creede are the center of operations for the upper Rio Grande. Del Norte and South Fork are located on U.S. 160 west of Alamosa and about 20 and 40 miles east of Wolf Creek Pass. From South Fork, Colorado 149 follows the river northwest about 20 miles to Creede, providing easy access to the water. West of Creede, CO 149 swings north, and Forest Road 520, located about 18 miles west of Creede, provides access to the river below and above Rio Grande Reservoir.

Lodging is found in each of these three towns and on guest ranches along the river. Contact the chambers of commerce in Creede, (719) 658-2374, South Fork, (719) 873-5327, and Del Norte, (719) 657-2845 for more information. Popular Forest Service campgrounds are found along Colorado 149 between South Fork and Creede, 5 miles west of Creede, and along Forest Road 520 on the way to Rio Grande Reservoir.

The Rio Grande tumbles from Stony Pass on the Continental Divide, beginning its journey as a typical freestone headwater stream averaging about ten feet in width. The river is free-flowing for about 20 miles before it is impounded in Rio Grande Reservoir, which is sometimes referred to in the area by its old name of Farmers' Union Reservoir.

One couldn't ask for a lovelier spot to cast a fly. High ridges surrounding the canyon are patched with snow, bright green aspens, and grassy slopes, with cliffs and spires of volcanic rock cracking the greenery. The stream is brush-lined, and casting is best done from the middle of the stream. Hip boots and short rods are in order on this stretch, and small high-floating attractor flies are effective. It is Humpy, Royal Wulff, or Irresistible water, and beadhead nymphs are effective in deep channels and pockets. Wild browns, rainbows, and a few cutthroats up to 16 inches present excellent fly-fishing opportunity.

To reach the upper river, take Forest Road 520 beyond River Hill Campground and Rio Grande Reservoir, about 50 miles west of Creede. Beyond the reservoir, Ute Creek Trailhead near Lost Trail Campground offers access to about a mile of river upstream, to a parcel of private land. Beyond the Lost Trail Campground, Forest Road 520 becomes a rough four-wheel-drive road that leads to many more miles of fishing opportunities. The road climbs a steep hill before dropping back to river level at Brewster Park in 2 miles. From here the road stays close to the canyon bottom and the river for 3 miles before climbing away on its route to Stony Pass. The fishable stretches of the headwaters are accessible by mountain bike on Forest Road 520.

Ute and Weminuche Creeks are two large headwaters of the Rio Grande, both fine trout streams. Located in the Weminuche Wilderness, they are accessible by trail only. Hike in from the Ute Creek Trailhead at the west end of Rio Grande Reservoir or from below the dam on the Weminuche Creek Trail. On Ute Creek, a one-mile hike leads to the stream, which is below the trail in a steep canyon. Farther upstream the valley opens to provide meadow fly fishing for small rainbows, brook trout, and cutthroats. The hike to Weminuche Creek is a bit longer but offers several miles of meadow fishing below Weminuche Pass.

From the Rio Grande Reservoir dam downstream to River Hill the Rio Grande is a short walk from the road. The river is twenty to thirty feet wide with a riffle-and-pool structure and lots of deep channels. For the first 2 miles below the dam the river frequently splits into several channels as it meanders through the willows and grasses. Despite the proximity of two campgrounds, fly fishing here can be excellent. Many shallow stretches are located in this stretch, but along cliffs the river may be up to eight feet deep. The clear water flows over a cobble and gravel bottom. Willows line the banks, but casting is easy from gravel bars and from within the stream.

Shallow water may be barren of fish, but the deep runs hold large wily rainbows and browns. These trout, living so close to the road, are well educated, and it requires carefully selected patterns to catch them. This stretch is mayfly and stonefly water. Salmon flies and golden stones come off from mid-June to late July depending on water temperatures and runoff conditions. Fish stonefly nymphs—Bitch Creek, Kaufmann's Stone, or Woven Stonefly—along the bottoms of riffles, in deep runs, and against cliffs. Mayfly hatches can be prolific through July and early August. Instead of a Royal Wulff, use a Parachute Adams, a Grizzly Wulff, or ginger-bodied mayfly imitations in sizes 12 to 18. Evening is particularly good in this stretch. Fish caddis patterns or flies with some white—Royal Humpy, House and Lot, or a Renegade, all in sizes 12 to 14—in slack water, current seams, and along the bank.

Below River Hill the Rio Grande cuts across a piece of the Weminuche Wilderness and dives into Box Canyon (sometimes called Six Mile Canyon). This is a wild, rocky stretch of river with no maintained trails leading into the canyon. Anglers must fight through a thicket to reach the river. The narrow canyon makes access impossible during periods of high flow. Stay out of this canyon during runoff. Keep in mind that this is a wild place filled with potential hazards, and help is a long way off.

Anglers can descend into Box Canyon from River Hill on Forest Road 520 or walk downstream 2 miles from River Hill Campground. Access to the lower end of the canyon is off Forest Road 520 about one mile from Colorado 149. Turn off Forest Road 520 onto Forest Road 21, which crosses 1.5 miles of private land to a trailhead in a group of cabins. When using this road be sure to close all gates.

Box Canyon presents a memorable scene from Forest Road 520. This stretch starts gently in a wide bottom, then narrows to swift and dangerous water below. Freestone and pocket water support large fish that are protected by the difficult access. Pools and pockets up to eight feet deep break the cascade. Plenty of deep water is found in this stretch, and pools hold large fish that don't see many fishermen. Note that a box canyon about halfway through will block your progress up- or downstream.

Hip waders are ideal for this stretch, where mobility is important. A four-piece rod will made the walk into the canyon easier. Like all pocket water, Box Canyon is best fished with big dry flies, weighted nymphs, or light soft-hackle patterns. Dry flies with heavy hackle or hair bodies will stand up well against the tumbling water. Irresistibles, Stimulators, Humpys, and Royal Wulffs are designed for this type of water. For subsurface fishing, weighted stonefly nymphs, beadheads, or Prince Nymphs are good choices.

Walk in as far as you like, then fish your way back, boulder-hopping and walking the banks. Make short casts into the pockets, around boulders, and into the heads of plunge pools. Both browns and rainbows are plentiful, but hooking and landing them in the turbulent currents will challenge even the most experienced fly fisherman.

Between Box Canyon and the town of South Fork, the Rio Grande flows first across a broad valley surrounded by high mountains, then through a narrow canyon. Colorado 149 closely parallels the river most of the way, providing easy access to it. However, much of the river is on private land. Within this stretch, fishing regulations vary. From the upper boundary of the Rio Grande Fisherman Access Area to the upper boundary of the Marshall Park Campground, angling is restricted to flies and lures only. The water is catch-and-release for all rainbows, and a two-fish bag and possession limit for brown trout is in effect. The browns must be 12 inches or shorter. The same regulations apply to the private water between Willow Creek and Goose Creek. From the Coller Bridge downstream to the west fence of Masonic Park, angling is fly and lure only. All rainbow trout must be immediately released back to the water. A two-fish limit on browns is in effect, and the browns must be over 16 inches. To avoid problems with private land and regulations, get a copy of the pamphlet *Fishing the Rio Grande* from the Monte Vista office of Colorado Department of Wildlife, (719) 852-4783. It contains a detailed map of landownership and where specific regulations apply.

Public access to 2 miles of river is found at the Rio Grande Fisherman Area off Colorado 149, 7 miles west of Creede at the old Rio Grande Campground. Another mile of access surrounds Marshall Creek Campground about 5 miles from Creede. On the downstream side of Wagon Wheel Gap, a long stretch of public water begins near Palisade Campground and continues about 8 miles east through the Coller State Wildlife Area. Keep in mind that the river along Colorado 149 sees a lot of pressure, and anglers must share the stream with other fishermen. Fortunately, one doesn't need much of a stretch of river to keep busy. Hundreds of likely spots invite a cast, and a quarter-mile of stream will provide a leisurely half-day of fishing.

An excellent way to fish this stretch of the Rio Grande is to stay at one of the many guest ranches from Wagon Wheel Gap to above Creede that offer fishing privileges. The private water holds fine populations of trout and thinner populations of anglers. The fly-fishing on the Wason, (719) 658-2413, and 4 UR, (719) 658-2202, ranches have a particularly fine reputation, but you must make reservations for these popular spots well in advance. Contact the Creede Chamber of Commerce at (719) 658-2374 for more information.

Throughout this long stretch, the Rio Grande is a midsized river, from forty to sixty feet wide with a classic riffle-run-pool structure. Depths range from one to six feet with plenty of deep runs and holes. The surface is often broken with boulders and there are plenty of pockets to hold fish. At Wagon Wheel Gap the current is swift, but it slows as the river approaches South Fork. Anglers will find the Rio Grande holds strong rainbows and fat browns. Most fish are in the 9- to 18-inch range, with many fish over 14 inches.

In this big water chest waders are required. Wading is tricky in the swift current and on the uneven bottom. Cobbles and boulders on the bottom make for difficult footing, and frequent drop-offs into deeper water require caution of all anglers. Casting is easy from gravel bars and from midstream, and brush is never a problem. Summer afternoons are often windy in Wagon Wheel Gap, so bring a long rod.

A long rod will help with fly presentation on the intricate currents of the upper Rio Grande. In-stream rocks and churning flows make a drag-free float difficult. To achieve the best drift, limit the length of line on the water. Make short casts and lift the line off the water with a long rod, keeping only the leader on or in the water. Slack-line casts are important. When casting across the currents use the rod tip to create waves in the line, or use S, curve, and reach casts.

Search for trout behind and in front of boulders and in deep runs and pockets. Surprisingly large trout can be plucked from deep channels within five feet of the bank. Rainbows are often found at midstream in the pockets and along the bottoms of runs; browns prefer the stream edges, particularly beneath overhanging vegetation.

Near Wagon Wheel Gap, the pocket water on the Rio Grande holds plenty of strong brown and rainbow trout. (Photograph by June Fabryka-Martin.)

The Rio Grande is home to abundant stoneflies, and the salmon fly hatch of mid- to late June can be heavy. Although the hatch may occur during runoff, the water is clear enough to permit dry-fly fishing. Fish the hatch with adult stonefly patterns such as the Sofa Pillow, Bird's Stone, or large Stimulators. Splashy casts that disturb the surface will often bring a vicious strike. Stonefly nymph patterns, especially the Bitch Creek, Brooks Stone, and the Woven Stone, are a good choice all season long. Use size 6 to 10 patterns with additional weight to get them deep in the fast runs.

The trout in this big water are not very fussy, and traditional big-water western patterns like the Humpy and Royal Wulff will often produce, as will flies more carefully matched to naturals. Attractors such as Elk Hair Caddis, Dry Muddler, and Royal Wulff work well throughout the afternoon and evening. Keep flies large enough to be easily spotted in the fast, choppy currents. A size 10 or 12 fly will work well, particularly on cloudy afternoons. Late in the summer or in quieter stretches of water the same patterns in smaller sizes, or a size 12 or 14 Parachute Adams, will often bring a trout out of hiding.

As the river meanders out into the San Luis Valley between South Fork and Del Norte, the Rio Grande is classified as Gold Medal Water. It is water that truly deserves its lasting reputation as a brown trout fishery, with many fine fish up to 16 inches. Some rainbows are also found here. The river is so rich that on a good day a skillful angler might catch ten fish without moving from a single spot. This stretch is fly and lure only, with a catch-and-release regulation for rainbows and a two-fish limit on browns, which must be over 16 inches.

Out of the mountains and canyons the river slows near South Fork and widens up to one hundred feet as it flows through agricultural land. The currents are generally slow as the river pushes through deep runs with occasional riffles and deep channels. Stream banks vary from grassy to willow- and tree-lined. Casting is obstruction-free from within the river. Getting to the stream is frequently easy, but deep runs at stream bends can force you to cast from the banks. Wading is usually no problem, but always keep in mind that this is big water and remain watchful of sudden drop-offs to deep water.

Brown trout swim the Rio Grande in incredible numbers, and fish are found everywhere. Browns are particularly fond of holding in deeper water near the banks and under the roots of willows in slow-moving water. In choppy runs about a foot deep trout will hold in the rocks on the bottom, freely rising to dry flies or taking nymphs at any depth. Look for current seams where a slow current passes against a faster one. Good fish can be taken from lies within a rod's length from where you are standing. Be watchful for hidden deep runs where large nymphs can snare a good-sized brown.

Most of this stretch is on private land, but state leases open several miles of stream bank to anglers. Anglers who wish to wade the Gold Medal Water will find access surrounding two bridges on County Roads 17 and 18 over the Rio Grande from U.S. 160. Current leases are posted at the access points. Check on the latest access information before fishing from any of the bridges. Easy access is found at County Road 18, where the north side of the river is open from Granger Bridge 2 miles upstream, and downstream to County Road 17. From Twin Mountain Bridge on County Road 17, easy access is on both banks of the river.

Because of the size of the river and the many stretches of private property that require permission to fish, floating this stretch with an experienced guide is an excellent way to get into some large browns. The river is floatable from above Creede to Twin Mountain Bridge. With numerous access points you can plan a wide variety of trips ranging from a half-day to two days.

Before mid-June the river is generally too cold for good fishing, and after August 1 the river is too low to float. Float trips are especially desirable during the early summer, when the river is fishable but still running high. During this time the river is awkward to wade but perfect for floating. Casting into the holding water along the bank from midstream is the easiest way to reach the trout during high flows. In addition, the floating season coincides with the timing of major hatches on the river. One can float and cast salmon flies, Golden Stones, Green Drakes, and caddis to rising trout all day.

To arrange a guided float trip, contact the Wason Ranch at (719) 658-2413, Gunnison River Expeditions at (970) 249-4441, or Duranglers at (970) 385-4081.

The incredible hatches of mayflies on the Gold Medal Water makes mid-June to late July a prime time for float or wade fishermen to plan a trip there. Green drakes, slate-winged duns, pale morning duns, and a large red quill are important through early August. Fish the hatches with high-floating mayfly imitations—Green and Brown Wulffs and Parachute Adams—in sizes 10 to 14. Caddis patterns are effective in the afternoons and evenings all summer long. On overcast days, fishing dry flies can produce almost constant action.

Even when hatches are thin, large dry flies bring the browns to the surface. Traditional western patterns will do the trick: size 10 to 12 Royal Wulffs, House and Lot Variants, Royal Trudes, Elk Hair Caddises, and Stimulators. Use these attractors to prospect for fish just about anywhere in the stream.

The Gold Medal Water fishes well into the fall, when angling is most productive in the afternoon. Large beadhead, Peacock, and Pheasant Tail nymphs or streamers are your best bet. *Baetis* hatches occur on fall afternoons and you should fish the hatch with your favorite Blue-Winged Olive patterns.

Fed by a sprawling high-elevation watershed, the Rio Grande can experience a wide range of runoff patterns. Cold water temperatures and high flows usually keep fishing slow well into June, although the river just below Rio Grande Reservoir may be fishable at this time. Runoff on the entire river is usually clear, and anglers desperate for action can fish pockets of holding water along the river edge in late June through mid-July. High water subsides by late July.

If we had to limit ourselves to fish one stream for the rest of our lives, it would be the Rio Grande. The incredible variety of fishing experience to be had on the river always provides a new challenge or a different setting in which to cast a fly. Populations of strong, wild trout add to the lure of the river, so different in reality from the picture normally conjured by the words "Rio Grande."

SOUTH FORK
OF THE RIO GRANDE

Managed by: Rio Grande National Forest, private
Access by: Foot and vehicle
Altitude: 7,200 to 12,200 feet
Type of Water: Freestone stream with some pocket water
Best times: Mid-July to September
Hatches: Golden stoneflies, green drakes
Maps: USGS South Fork West, Beaver Creek Reservoir, and
   Mount Hope 7.7' quadrangles

The South Fork of the Rio Grande is the largest tributary of
the main river draining from the San Juans in Colorado. Averaging fifteen to twenty feet in width, the South Fork is a
good-sized river and one certainly worthy of the angler's attention. The South Fork heads against the ridge on the north
side of Wolf Creek Pass, an area that receives monumental
amounts of snow each winter. The lower half of the river is
paralleled by roads, creating easy access not found on many
streams in southern Colorado. Thick insect hatches, clear
conditions, over 20 miles of public water, and several interesting tributaries add to the attraction.

The main stretch of the South Fork lies beside U.S. 160
between the town of South Fork and Wolf Creek Pass. The
first 2 miles above town are private, and the public stretch of
water above is broken in three places by well-marked private
parcels. Public water is found surrounding Highway Springs
and Park Creek Campgrounds and above the gate that closes
the pass during severe winter storms. At the junction with
Pass Creek, South Fork leaves the highway and is paralleled
by the all-weather gravel Forest Road 410 for 2 miles to Big
Meadows Reservoir. Ample pull-offs are available along each
of the roads, and special fishermen's parking is located at the

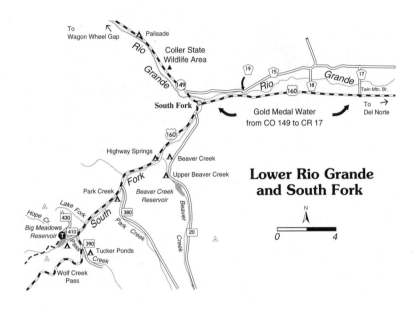

Lower Rio Grande
and South Fork

junction of Forest Road 410 and U.S. 160 and 7 miles up from South Fork at the junction with Forest Road 380.

The headwaters of the South Fork pass through a rugged glacial valley before being impounded in Big Meadow Reservoir. The upper stretch of the river is a tumbling freestone stream less than ten feet wide. For most of its length it is lined with thick willows, and it often crashes through narrow rocky gorges. It is tough but interesting fishing for small rainbows and brook trout. Choppy currents require the use of high-visibility flies such as House and Lot, Renegade, and Royal Humpys, so take a big selection of your favorites. Streamers fished deep are also effective at the small point of land where the river dumps into the reservoir.

Reach the upper South Fork by taking Forest Road 410 from U.S. 160 for 2 miles and heading for the Archuleta Trailhead near the dam. The trail leads around the lake in 1 mile to parallel the river for about 3 miles. The reservoir itself holds small rainbows and brook trout.

After collecting the water from its South Fork, the Rio Grande is over one hundred feet wide and provides plenty of current seams for trout to feed along. (Photograph by Craig Martin.)

Below Big Meadows Reservoir South Fork is a high-gradient stream ten to fifteen feet wide, gaining breadth downstream to a maximum of about twenty-five feet. Freestone water most of the way, the river flows through a narrow canyon. Rocky cliffs often pinch the stream to flow through short gorges where the water drops as much as a hundred feet. Short sections of pocket water are also found, as are deeper runs with a smooth surface. Calmer water is located in the wide sections of canyon where the campgrounds are located, and rough water is found along the parts of the canyon that are just wide enough for the road and stream.

There is plenty of deep holding water in the river, and it is here anglers will want to concentrate their efforts. Trout often lie in smooth slicks against the banks and in pockets lying between current-breaking boulders. The river is frequently broken into two or more channels, and trout will often sit in the deeper water just below where the channels rejoin. An abundance of smaller fish are found in the long riffles.

Drive along the road, pick a spot that strikes your fancy, and work upstream. Steep banks near the road are sometimes an annoyance but can easily be bypassed. Casting is easy from within the stream, but streamside firs and willows are always a hazard to your backcast. After runoff wading is easy along the banks, but the swift currents and a few sudden drop-offs require caution. Shallow water that offers easy wading is often found near the banks, making it possible to cast from midstream. The cobbles of the stream bottom are rounded and slick, so felt-soled wading shoes are an asset. Wet wading is possible in summer. A short rod, 8 feet or less, works well. Bring 3- or 4-weight fly line and short, 7- to 9-foot, leaders.

Evening is the best time to be on the water. The sun will be at your back, heavy caddis hatches will be on the water, and rising trout will be in all directions. Often you will be forced to cast into a pocket of slack water that lies beyond the faster currents of the main flow. Use reach and slack-line casts to get the fly to the target, then try to get as much line off the water as possible. It takes only a couple of seconds of float to induce a trout to strike.

South Fork holds brown, rainbow, and brook trout. Browns are dominant in the lower river but remain present to Big Meadows Reservoir. Brook trout are found above Park Creek Campground, and rainbows are found in the entire river. Most fish are 9 inches or less, but each section holds trout up to 14 inches.

Insects produced in the clean, well-oxygenated water keep the trout in South Fork actively feeding. Golden stoneflies hatch in early to mid-July, and Bucktail Caddis, Elk Hair Caddis, or Stimulator patterns, sizes 10 to 12, often bring slashing strikes from trout in swift water. Around the same time, a reliable caddis hatch occurs in the evening. Use a tan-bodied Elk Hair Caddis in sizes 12 to 14 to fish along the banks, or float a Goddard Caddis through the riffles and along the edges of slack currents at midstream. A variety of mayflies are almost always on the water. A dark-winged green drake hatch occurs in late July when size 10 or 12 Green Wulffs, Green Humpys, or other green drake patterns are effective in fast water. Good hatches of pale evening duns occur in late July and early August. In the afternoon or evening, cast a Light Cahill or a PMD Comparadun, size 14 or 16, to rising fish. In the late season try casting your favorite grasshopper pattern tight up against the banks of the meadow reaches.

Four tributaries of the South Fork are worth a try. Hope Creek and Lake Fork are small streams accessible from Forest Road 430 just north of Big Meadows Reservoir. Trails parallel both streams, which offer wilderness fly fishing for small brook and cutthroat trout. Closer to the town of South Fork, Beaver Creek is reached via Forest Road 20 about a mile south of town on U.S. 160. Above the Beaver Creek Campgrounds Forest Road 20 parallels the stream for about 10 miles, interrupted by Beaver Creek Reservoir and a parcel of private land above the impoundment. Beaver Creek offers fine small-stream fly fishing for good-sized browns and rainbows.

An interesting tributary of South Fork is Pass Creek. The confluence lies at the intersection of Forest Road 410 and U.S. 160 a few miles below Wolf Creek Pass. Just upstream from the confluence, Pass Creek jumps through a narrow gorge with several access points from U.S. 160. The pocket water holds good-sized browns and rainbows. Use high-floating flies and be cautious of fast water and sudden drop-offs in the narrow canyon.

The upper section of Pass Creek is paralleled by Forest Road 390 for 6 miles. Here the stream flows through alternating wide meadows and narrow granite gorges. Working your way upstream can be difficult because willows and cliffs block the way. By carefully choosing a point by which to descend from the road to the river, you can fish uninterrupted for a couple of hours. This freestone water is about ten feet wide and flows through usually thick streamside vegetation. There is plenty of deep water to hold trout, and browns, brookies, and a few rainbows, all up to 14 inches, are found here. Rio Grande cutthroats swim in the headwaters. Wading is easy on the cobbles of the bottom; casting from within the stream will help eliminate snags on the streamside vegetation.

Hatches are sporadic at 9,500 feet, and the trout of Pass Creek are opportunistic feeders. No need to be fancy here: Along the banks and in the wide bends use a Parachute Adams, a Royal Wulff, or your favorite realistic attractor; a Humpy or Irresistible in sizes 10 to 14 will be adequate in the riffles and pocket water.

6

THE SAN JUAN WATERSHED

UPPER FORKS
OF THE SAN JUAN RIVER

Managed by: San Juan National Forest, Weminuche Wilderness

Access by: Vehicle, foot, and mountain bike

Altitude: 7,700 to 12,100 feet

Type of Water: Freestone, pocket water, rugged canyons

Best Times: July to September

Hatches: Golden stoneflies, mayflies, caddis

Maps: USFS San Juan National Forest; USGS Wolf Creek Pass, Elwood Pass, Saddle Mountain, South River Peak 7.5' quadrangles

In 1765, Juan Rivera was commissioned by the Spanish governor of New Mexico to push northwestward from Taos to search for minerals and to make contact with the Native Americans in what is now southern Colorado. Rivera's diary reveals he reached a new river on the eve of *La Dia de San Juan*. Saint John was Rivera's patron saint, and he named the river and the mountains from which it flowed "San Juan."

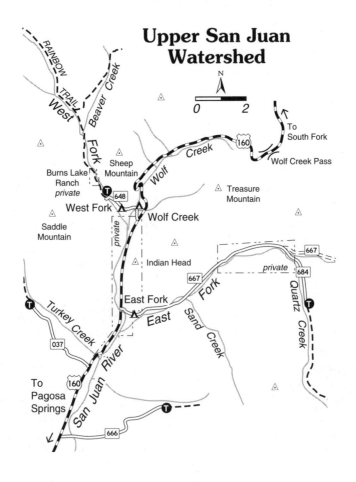

Upper San Juan Watershed

The San Juan River is a major tributary of the Colorado River and one of the largest rivers draining the mountains that share its name. It heads in the high country south of Wolf Creek Pass where spectacular peaks and glacial valleys provide a dramatic backdrop to the river. The San Juan then flows west and south into New Mexico, where it is impounded by Navajo Dam, creating a world-class tailwater fishery. Below, the San Juan becomes a desert river, carving deep canyons before joining the Colorado River at Lake Powell in Utah.

Unfortunately for anglers, most of the San Juan in Colorado flows through private land and the Southern Ute Indian Reservation. Thus, fishing opportunities on the main river are limited. A short stretch of public water is found within the town of Pagosa Springs, and it offers the real possibility of landing a 20-inch trout within the town limits. (Note that from the east end of town to Apache Street a bag and possession limit of two fish is in effect for all anglers.) Below Pagosa Springs floating is the only way to fish the river, but land ownership is often unclear and access is tricky. Most of the river on the Southern Ute Reservation flows through allotted lands and is off-limits to anglers.

All is not lost, however, for the two main forks of the upper San Juan are delightful small trout streams. The East and West Forks of the San Juan are a pair of complementary streams. The East Fork is a tumbling freestone stream, and there is easy access to 6 miles of river by graded road. For the more adventurous, the West Fork offers endless hike-in water deep in the Weminuche Wilderness in rugged canyons and peaceful meadows. In general, the East Fork is easier to fly fish, and the West Fork offers more adventure and solitude. Neither stream is a producer of large fish, but they are consistently good for small trout.

The forks join to form the main San Juan River about 9 miles northeast of Pagosa Springs. Ten miles east of Pagosa Springs on U.S. 160, a well-marked graded road follows the

East Fork through its canyon. The first 5 miles of Forest Road 667 is an easy trip for passenger cars, making the East Fork an ideal backcountry adventure accessible by car. Four miles beyond the East Fork on U.S. 160 at the foot of the steep ascent to Wolf Creek Pass, Forest Road 648 provides access to the West Fork. Quiet Forest Service campgrounds are located on both rivers, and plenty of primitive campsites are found along the East Fork. Backpacking opportunities along the West Fork beyond Burns Lake Ranch extend over 10 miles upstream into the heart of the Weminuche Wilderness. The nearest services to both forks are located in Pagosa Springs, and some lodging is available near the forks at the foot of Wolf Creek Pass.

The lower miles of both forks hold populations of brown and rainbow trout. Fish remain on the small side, ranging from 7 to 12 inches. The forks hold small cutthroat trout in their upper miles. The lower miles of the East Fork receive heavy fishing pressure, and one must work the water thoroughly to find good-sized fish. Many anglers try the water near West Fork Campground, but the wilderness section of the West Fork receives light pressure.

The East Fork is paralleled by Forest Road 667. The gravel road perches on the slope directly above the stream, making frequent dips to river level. Public access to the river begins at the East Fork Campground and continues 5 miles upstream to a well-marked parcel of private land. Throughout this stretch the road is a wide single lane. Use good judgment when stopping along the road, and park only in safe pull-outs where the road widens. A 4-mile stretch of river flows on private land and is closed to anglers. Above the private land anglers can choose either of two headwater streams: the main East Fork, which is paralleled by the four-wheel-drive Forest Road 667 that climbs Elwood Pass; or turn onto Forest Road 684, which climbs the valley of Quartz Creek. This steep road requires four-wheel drive and can make an excellent mountain bike trip. Note that high water can block access to Quartz

Below its remote and rugged canyon, the West Fork of the San Juan River flows through a flat-bottom glacial valley at the western foot of Wolf Creek Pass. (Photograph by Craig Martin.)

Creek from the ford of the East Fork near the beginning of Forest Road 684 in spring and early summer.

The lowermost miles of the East Fork tumble through a rocky gorge. The stream is pocket water with large boulders, deep plunge pools, and small waterfalls. It is about twenty to twenty-five feet wide with a cobble bottom. In most places the stream is wadable, but anglers should wear felts and use caution in the swift water. The canyon is heavily forested with large Douglas firs growing on the stream banks. It is difficult to work along the stream on the banks. Casting from the banks is difficult due to the thick vegetation, but in the river casting is easy. For this stream, 7½- to 8-foot rods are appropriate.

About 2 miles up from the campground the East Fork drops through a series of falls where fishing is difficult. Calmer water begins above the junction with Sand Creek. From here to the boundary of private land the river is comprised of long riffles and runs flowing through small meadows with spotty streamside willows and alders. Angling is much easier in this stretch than in the pocket water below. The river in this stretch is about 12 feet wide. Above the private land, the East Fork and Quartz Creek are small streams that offer fine wilderness fishing.

The roily water of the lower East Fork is stonefly territory. Golden stoneflies hatch in early July, often during the final stages of runoff. When the water is clear, fishing size 10 or 12 Stimulators in slack pockets under overhanging vegetation is an excellent way to take trout. Throughout the year, weighted stonefly nymphs fished along the bottom are effective. Size 12 to 16 nymphs that imitate smaller stoneflies are also good choices. Try the Prince Nymph, All Purpose Black, or Brooks Stone. Float nymphs through the slack-water pockets, around boulders, and into the heads of plunge pools. Be patient. It may take a half-dozen casts to a single location to lure a trout.

For the remainder of the summer the East Fork is a caddisfly stream. Hatches occur most afternoons and offer the best fishing of the day. Anytime after 4 P.M., cast a good floating caddis pattern such as Elk Hair Caddis, Royal Trude, or Goddard Caddis along the banks. Sizes vary with the hatch, ranging from 12 to 16. In general, larger sizes are good early in the season and smaller flies are more effective later in the year. Skittering the pattern across the surface is a fine technique for taking trout. Caddis larva patterns like Green Rock Worms in 10 to 14 are also a good choice. Fishing soft-hackle patterns, particularly a Green-and-Partridge, is an excellent way to catch fish during a hatch.

In the meadow sections of the East Fork terrestrials become important. Hopper, cricket, and ant patterns are all effective from mid-July through September. Fish often hold along the banks waiting for insects to drop into the water. Hopper patterns can be cast with a splash to disturb the surface of the water and alert fish to their presence. Floating hoppers as wet flies just below the surface is another effective technique. Traditional hoppers like a Dave's or Joe's Hopper in sizes 10 to 14 are good choices. Also effective is the rubber-legged Madam X.

Access to and angling on the West Fork of the San Juan is more difficult. From its junction with the East Fork, the West Fork flows through a lovely valley on private land. As the river turns west into the mountains, Forest Road 648 leads to West Fork Campground and the beginning of public water. The road offers easy access to the river for a half-mile above the campground. Just above the Forest Road 648 bridge over the West Fork is a half-mile of public water with difficult access. The river flows through a dramatic canyon with steep cliffs and a rugged floor. The way upstream is often blocked by large rocks. A parcel of private land blocks further progress along the stream.

The majority of the West Fork is accessible only by trail. About 12 miles of river are above the bridge on Forest Road 648. The glacial valley of the West Fork is one of the most spectacular locations in the San Juans, with hot springs and numerous waterfalls adding to the attraction. The upper river is reached via the Rainbow Trail. The trailhead is just above the bridge on Forest Road 648. The first mile of the trail passes through private land, so observe the frequent posted warnings and stay on the trail. The trail remains high above the stream for the first 3 miles, dropping to a footbridge across the West Fork near Beaver Creek. From here upstream, short stretches of meadow and pocket water are accessible. Most of the trail, however, remains high above the tumbling stream.

The gradient of the West Fork is steeper than that of the East Fork, and the towering walls above the stream shed huge boulders that break up the flow. The result is superb pocket water and long riffles. The stream is ten to twenty feet wide, with a clean cobble and boulder bottom. Wading can be difficult on the West Fork and anglers must use caution. Swift currents and streamside vegetation combine to make angling difficult. This is not a place for beginning fly fishermen.

Some stoneflies and caddis are found on the West Fork, but mayflies are important on this stream. Slate-winged drakes hatch in July and can offer some fine dry-fly fishing. Use a size 10 or 12 Green or Brown Wulff with heavy grizzly hackle to withstand the choppy currents. Cast to rising fish, or use the fly as an attractor to find hidden trout. Many trout lie in pockets. Cast into the small pillows of slack water, keeping as much fly line off the water as possible. This requires fishing mostly with leader and tippet, keeping the rod high in the air.

The volcanic rocks of the upper San Juan watershed make both forks susceptible to off-color runoff. Murky conditions turn the water to chalky brown. High water begins in late April and continues through early July or may end in mid-June in years with low snowpack. In years with high snowpack—not an unusual occurrence in the vicinity of Wolf Creek Pass—these streams may not be fishable until mid-July. Heavy summer thunderstorms can muddy the East Fork for a couple of days in midsummer.

For those seeking small-stream wilderness fly fishing, the upper San Juan watershed has plenty to offer. Coal Creek is reached from U.S. 160 on the gravel Fawn Gulch Road about 4 miles north of Pagosa Springs. Go about 5 miles east on Forest Road 666 to the Coal Creek Trailhead. The trail follows the stream for 3 miles, offering tough fishing in pocket water for small rainbows and cutthroats. Sand Creek lies 3 miles from U.S. 160 on Forest Road 667 in the canyon of the East Fork. Anglers who don't mind some rugged hiking upstream will find tumbling freestone water with fine caddis hatches and a heavy hatch of black quills in late July. The Turkey Creek Trail provides access to a 7-mile stretch of Turkey Creek, mostly in the Weminuche Wilderness. Reach the trailhead about 4 miles up Forest Road 37 (Jackson Mountain Road), about 7 miles north of Pagosa Springs on U.S. 160. Near the trailhead the trail and stream cross private land,

and you must walk about a mile before you can fish. Beyond that point the trail stays close to the creek for 8 miles. Tumbling Turkey Creek holds small rainbows and cutthroats, and the valley offers an eyeful of fine scenery.

SAN JUAN RIVER BELOW NAVAJO DAM

Managed by: New Mexico State Parks
Access by: Vehicle
Altitude: 5,600 to 5,700 feet
Type of Water: Tailwater
Best Times: All year
Hatches: Midges, caddis, blue-winged olive, pale morning dun
Maps: USGS Navajo Dam and Archuleta 7.5' quadrangles

Only 60 miles south of Durango, the world-class tailwater fishery on the San Juan River below Navajo Dam is easily accessible to southern Colorado fly fishers. After heading in the mountains surrounding Wolf Creek Pass and flowing through Pagosa Springs, the San Juan flows into Navajo Reservoir. Almost 40 miles of the river lie impounded by Navajo Dam, which lies below the border in New Mexico. Outflow from the dam is from the bottom of the lake, a situation that puts a constant flow of cold water into the river below, creating a marvelous trout stream.

In contrast to most of the mountain fishing in Colorado, the San Juan in New Mexico flows through the high desert. About 20 miles of the San Juan are a viable trout fishery, and of this, only 5 five miles have easy access and are regularly fished. The situation gives the San Juan another contrast to mountain fishing: hoards of anglers. If you are looking for

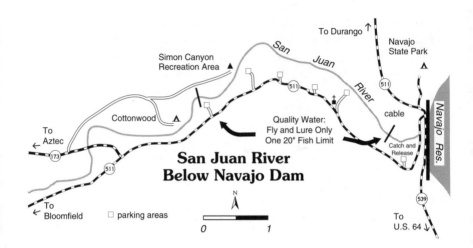

San Juan River
Below Navajo Dam

solitude, this section of the San Juan is not for you. But if you are looking for the chance for easy access to large rainbows, the San Juan is hard to beat.

From Durango, the Navajo Dam is reached via U.S. 550 south. From the south end of Durango, take U.S. 160/550 south. In 5 miles bear right onto U.S. 550 south, heading toward Aztec. Continue for 35 miles, crossing the New Mexico border, to Aztec, then turn left onto New Mexico 173. In 20 miles turn left onto New Mexico 511. Access to the stream is easy from this intersection to the dam, about 5 miles ahead.

Outflow from the dam keeps water temperatures nearly constant at 42 degrees Fahrenheit. The fishery is carefully managed for rainbow trout. Rainbows are stocked as fingerlings, growing up as near-wild fish that can grow to over 22 inches. Snake River cutthroats were once stocked in the San Juan, and cutbow hybrids are occasionally caught here. Brown trout are unusual but may be found in the lower reaches of the Quality Water. Although the number of large fish may have declined over the last decade, anglers will still catch their share of large-sized trout.

To enhance the quality of fishing on the San Juan, New Mexico Department of Game and Fish has special regulations in place for the water below the dam. The first quarter-mile below the dam is fly and lure, barbless hook, catch-and-release water. The lower boundary is marked by a cable stretching across the river. The next 3.5 miles of the river is known as the Quality Water. Angling is limited to artificial flies and lures with single barbless hooks, and anglers may take only one trout of at least 20 inches. Once you have a trout in your possession, you must stop fishing.

Below Navajo Dam the San Juan is a large low-gradient river over one hundred feet wide. The river flows through a shallow canyon with scattered vegetation on the canyon floor, like a spring creek in the desert. Willows are common along the banks and in the islands of the river. The stream is often channelized in shallow stretches, but deep runs are found almost everywhere. The flow ranges from 500 cubic feet per second (cfs) to 5,000 cfs, with optimum amounts from 600 to 1,200 cfs. High spring flows can vary depending on mountain snowpack and reservoir conditions. Seasonal fluctuations are to be expected, but flows do not normally change on a daily basis as in many tailwaters.

Like any other large western river, wading the San Juan during high flows can be extremely dangerous. In high water wadable areas are available, but they are less numerous than at lower flows. It is certain that wading in high flows is not for the first-time visitor to the San Juan. Always use extreme caution when wading this river.

Cold water temperatures require that anglers wear neoprene chest waders at all times. Prolific algae growth makes for slippery footing throughout the river. Additional dangers are found in the irregular stream bottom that hides deep holes and long eroded slots. Felt-soled wading shoes are essential equipment for fishing here, and chest waders should always be used with a wading belt to prevent water from flowing into your waders in case of a fall.

The size of the water dictates the use of rods at least 9 feet long, especially for mending line on long floats on quiet water.

Because most fishing here involves small flies, 4- to 6-weight lines are best. Nine-foot leaders and heavy tippet can be used for fishing San Juan Worms and leech imitations, but many situations on the river call for 12-foot 5X to 7X leaders.

Many first-time visitors to the San Juan find it easier to fish the river with an experienced guide. Both wade and float trips are available from about thirty outfitters in Durango, Farmington, Santa Fe, and near the dam itself. Consult fly-fishing magazines or angling newsgroups on online services or the Internet for some suggestions on available and reliable guide service.

Near-constant flows and water temperatures create conditions on the San Juan that are quite different from nearby mountain streams. Trout are careful, selective feeders. Successful anglers come to the river prepared to match the size and color of the dominant food source for that day. Fortunately, only a limited number of insect species are found on the river.

Angling the San Juan is always a challenge. Presentations must be exact and drifts must be drag-free. The complex nature of San Juan fly fishing cannot be easily summarized in a few words. What follows is only an outline of the conditions and requirements of fly fishing this complex stretch of water.

Abundant midge hatches occur year-round, making midges the most important food source on the river. Fish feed on adult and immature insects as well as on mating clusters of insects. Midge larva and pupa patterns ranging from size 18 to 28 should be fished dead-drift at varying depths, including just below the surface. Dry-fly fishing with adult midge patterns can be effective, but if conditions are right, fishing midge cluster patterns may be more productive. Midge cluster flies are often simple black-thread bodies with a grizzly hackle tied parachute-style on a white post clipped short in sizes 14 or 16. When fish are freely rising to clusters, this type of pattern can make your day.

Mayflies are found in riffles and on the flats below the riffles. Spring and fall hatches of blue-winged olives provide some excellent dry-fly fishing, especially on calm cloudy after-noons. Trout will rise to size 18 or 20 Blue-Winged Olive pat-terns. From early July to late September pale morning dun hatches occur in early afternoon. The hatch is often better on sunny days. Fish with size 14 or 16 pale yellow Compara-duns. If the fish are taking emergers below the surface, a va-riety of rusty, dark PMD emerger patterns should do well.

Trout often take insects just below the surface. Come to the San Juan prepared to fish size 16 to 20 Pheasant Tail or dark Hare's Ear nymphs in the surface film. Sparsely tied RS2 and WD-40 nymphs, sizes 18 to 22, are also effective. Slight changes in coloration can make a big difference.

When no insect activity is observed, prospect for trout with subsurface patterns. Red, orange, tan, and brown San Juan Worms are effective year-round. Black or brown rabbit and marabou leeches in large sizes are a good choice in slow-moving water. Egg patterns are also popular on the river. You can find an incredible variety of patterns designed specifically for this river at local shops. Hot patterns come and go, so keep an open mind. Experiment, try something different, and don't be reluctant to ask for suggestions at the local hangouts.

You should have no trouble finding fish, for they are everywhere. Adapt your fishing techniques to the location you select. The flats, the channels, the pools, and the riffles all hold plenty of trout.

Even though the San Juan may not provide the experi-ence that each fly fisher may look for, it is a remarkable fish-ery that deserves at least a day trip by anglers visiting the area. The San Juan rarely disappoints experienced anglers or those who choose to go with a good guide. The popularity of the river, however, has made it increasingly difficult to enjoy an uncrowded stretch of the San Juan. During the peak season, from June to October, try to hit the river at midweek. From November to March the river can be delightful—dress warmly and you'll have a day like no other on the San Juan.

RIO BLANCO

Managed by: San Juan National Forest, South San Juan Wilderness Area
Access by: Vehicle and foot
Altitude: 7,100 to 10,200 feet
Type of Water: Freestone stream with pocket water, meadows
Best Times: Late July to October
Hatches: Mayflies, midges
Maps: USFS San Juan National Forest; USGS Serviceberry Mountain, Harris Lake, and Summit Peak 7.5' quadrangles

The Rio Blanco contrasts sharply with many other small tributaries of the San Juan River in Colorado. Rather than tumbling pocket water, it is a classic western freestone river. In its lower public sections the Rio Blanco has a low gradient, making it an easy, relaxing place to fly fish for trout. It meanders through a shallow canyon in a broad valley of easily eroded Mancos shale, creating turns against crumbling shale cliffs. Smaller than most other rivers in the area, the Blanco beckons with the promise of fun fishing for some nice fish. With so many other better-known rivers nearby, few anglers give the Blanco a try.

The Rio Blanco (also known as the Blanco River) heads in the South San Juan Wilderness Area just over the Continental Divide from the Conejos River. No roads or trails lead to the very headwaters, but a short section of the upper Rio Blanco is accessible from County Road 326 about 10 miles south of Pagosa Springs. Travel east about 15 miles to the trailhead for Trail 573 at the Hare Ranch. An easement through this private land leads to the river in about 2 miles.

Private land surrounds the river in the expansive Blanco Basin. At the lower end of the basin water is diverted from the

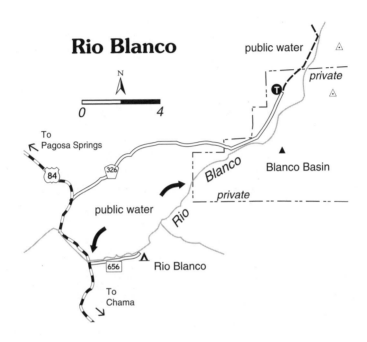

Blanco through a tunnel into the Navajo River drainage, and then flows via another long tunnel to Heron Lake in New Mexico. Farther below, from U.S. 84 west to the confluence with the San Juan, the Blanco flows across more private land. In between the private stretches lies a 10-mile stretch of river that is public water. Forest Road 656 parallels the Blanco for 3 miles above U.S. 84, offering easy access to the middle portion of the river. Above the Rio Blanco Campground at the end of Forest Road 656, the river stretches for many trailless miles, a place where adventurous fly fishermen will find long stretches of river to themselves.

The Rio Blanco is easily reached via U.S. 84 south of Pagosa Springs. Take U.S. 84 south from U.S. 160 at the east end of Pagosa. Continue about 10 miles south, cross the

Rio Blanco, and immediately turn left onto Forest Road 656. The road stays at river level for a short distance before climbing above the valley. In 3 miles the road ends at Rio Blanco Picnic Area and Campground, which is right on the river. Access to the river is upstream from U.S. 84 and at the picnic area and campground.

The Blanco is a small river, ranging from ten to twenty feet in width. It is a gently falling freestone stream with some pockets, long shallow riffles, and occasional deep channels along the banks. Many of the stream's bends are up against shale cliffs, at which points the river deepens to eight feet. The bottom is rounded cobbles with some interesting slate ledges. A wooded canyon surrounds the river, which is lined with willows.

The Blanco is shallow enough in most places to allow free access to any place on the stream. Wet wading is perfect for this stream, except in the fall when neoprene hip boots will ward off the chill from the water. Casting is never a problem on this river. It is easy to wade into position and cast from shallow water or from the many gravel bars along the main flow. In summer you can work up a couple miles of the stream, moving from bank to bank.

The size of the fish reflects the size of the stream. Anglers on the Blanco will find brown trout in the 7- to 12-inch range, with a few larger fish inhabiting the deeper runs against the cliffs. A few surprisingly large cutbows are also found in isolated sections of the river, and rainbows are scattered throughout. The Blanco is not a rich trout stream, and fish are not found everywhere. You will have to make plenty of casts before you come across a good trout.

Midsummer brings out a few species of clinger mayflies above the riffles, notably black quills and red quills. Midges occur in great numbers all summer long, and adult midge patterns are often a fine choice to fish in the quiet water along the banks in the evening. Most of the time anglers will have to rely on attractor patterns. Because these trout see few fishermen, patterns such as Royal Wulff, Humpy, and Elk Hair Caddis will catch fish. Much of the flow is smooth and unbroken, and more subtle patterns often work better. Try casting an Adams, Brown Wulff, Grizzly Wulff, or a Light Cahill, in sizes 12 to 16. Seek out the deeper water behind rocks, in pockets, in channels eroded into shale ledges, and in the deep holes along the cliffs. The riffles hold a few trout if the depth is over twelve inches. Cover the water thoroughly to find the hidden fish. In the deep channels, nymphs often work better than dry flies. Keep your choice of pattern small, no larger than size 12. Beadheaded Gold-Ribbed Hare's Ears sink well and are effective in the channels, as are olive, gray, and tan nymphs.

In midsummer, grasshoppers are the key to a successful day on the Blanco. Hoppers are abundant in the meadows and willows along the river, and the big insects attract the trout to the surface for a quick feast. Hopper patterns can be effective anywhere in the river. Try patterns from size 8 to 12. Joe's Hoppers, Deer Hoppers, or large Elk Hair Caddis will bring trout up from the bottoms of all but the deepest pools. In deep water, hoppers fished as wet flies are more effective than are those fished on the surface.

Because much of the Blanco watershed is found in the easily eroded Mancos shale, the Blanco is often off-color, a condition that no doubt led to the river's name. The gray muds of the shale give the river a chalky appearance during runoff and after heavy summer storms. Murkiness can remain in the river from late April through late July and for several days following rains in July, August, or even September. Fall, with the colorful cottonwoods and aspens surrounding the river, usually provides clear but low water conditions.

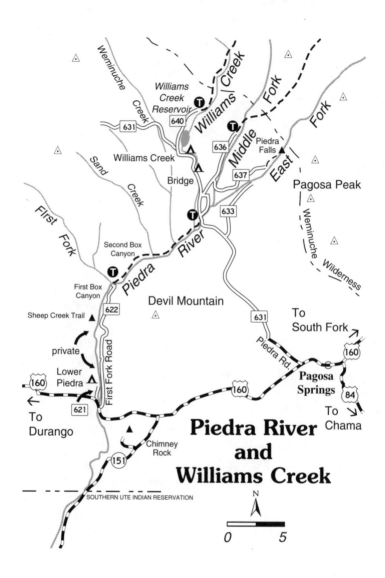

Williams Creek Reservoir

Weminuche Creek

Williams Creek

Middle Fork

East Fork

631

640

636

Piedra Falls

637

Williams Creek

Bridge

633

Sand Creek

First Fork

Second Box Canyon

Piedra River

First Box Canyon

Devil Mountain

Pagosa Peak

Weminuche Wilderness

Sheep Creek Trail

622

631

To South Fork

private

First Fork Road

Piedra Rd.

160

Lower Piedra

Pagosa Springs

84

160

621

160

To Durango

To Chama

Chimney Rock

151

Piedra River and Williams Creek

SOUTHERN UTE INDIAN RESERVATION

N

0   5

7

THE PIEDRA WATERSHED

PIEDRA RIVER

Managed by: San Juan National Forest, Weminuche Wilder-
   ness Area, Southern Ute Indian Reservation
Access by: Vehicle and foot
Altitude: 6,800 to 11,000 feet
Type of Water: Freestone stream, pocket water
Best Times: Late June to October
Hatches: Golden stoneflies, salmon flies, caddis, mayflies
Maps: USFS San Juan National Forest; USGS Cimarrona
   Peak, Oakbrush Ridge, Bear Mountain, Devil Mountain,
   Chimney Rock, and Allison 7.5' quadrangles

The Piedra River is one of our favorite streams in southern
Colorado. A small river flowing through granite box canyons
and tilting sedimentary rocks, the Piedra is more intimate than
most other streams draining the San Juans. The complex
stream structure and currents make each section of the Piedra
interesting and plucking trout from its waters challenging. Add
to that the fact that the Piedra is a wild stream with few miles
accessible by vehicle and you've got nearly perfect trout water.

The river derives its name from nearby Chimney Rock, a rock spire seen by modern travelers just south of U.S. 160 about 15 miles west of Pagosa Springs. Early Spanish explorers called the pinnacle *La Piedra Parada*, "The Standing Stone." Perhaps the Spanish simply translated an Indian name, for this landmark stood along a well-used Ute trail. The river flows within sight of the rock, and the stream acquired a shortened version of the name, *La Piedra*. Anglers with find the river is aptly named: Rockiness is the dominant characteristic of the entire stream.

The Piedra can be divided into three distinct sections. The headwaters drain from the Continental Divide in the Weminuche Wilderness. The East Fork of the Piedra is virtually inaccessible, flowing through a trailless forest above Piedra Falls; part of the Middle Fork of the Piedra is paralleled by Forest Road 636, but most of the stream lies in rugged canyons in the wilderness and can be explored only by strong hikers. Between Forest Road 631 to the east and U.S. 160 on the west, the main Piedra flows through a narrow 24- mile valley broken by two box canyons. This long stretch of hike-in water is the prime fly fishing section of the river. Below U.S. 160 the river flows across a broad valley on private land and the Southern Ute Indian Reservation.

Four points provide easy access to the Piedra. To reach the Middle Fork, take Piedra Road (County Road 600/Forest Road 631) north from U.S. 160 2 miles west of downtown Pagosa Springs. Continue on this all-weather gravel road about 17 miles to Forest Road 636 and bear right. After passing through a stretch of private land, the road parallels the Middle Fork for 4 miles before ending at the trailhead for the upper reaches of the Middle Fork. Forest Road 637 leads off Forest Road 636 to the East Fork, which is reached about 12 miles from Forest Road 631 at Piedra Falls.

The upper, northern end of the central-valley stretch of the Piedra is also reached via Piedra Road and Forest Road 631 out of Pagosa Springs. Take Forest Road 631 15 miles from U.S. 160 and park at the trailhead just beyond the bridge over the Piedra. From this point, Trail 596 parallels the Piedra for 12 miles through the canyon. The hike in from the upper end offers plenty of camping spots in the meadows along the river from Williams Creek west.

The lower end of the central section of the Piedra at the base of Devil Mountain is reached from U.S. 160 20 miles west of Pagosa Springs and about 40 miles east of Durango. A short stretch of public water is located near the Lower Piedra Campground off Forest Road 621 on the west side of the river. Follow the signs for the campground, and be aware that private land is located a half-mile above the campground.

To reach the central portion of the river, take First Fork Road (Forest Road 622). Just before the highway bridge over the Piedra on U.S. 160, First Fork Road heads north on the east bank of the river. This all-weather gravel road is suitable for all vehicles as it parallels the river for 12 miles from high above on the slopes of the canyon, dropping to river level only at the Piedra Bridge at the end of the road.

Along Forest Road 622 it's a steep 600-foot drop to the river from the road, and private land blocks access to the river in this stretch. Anglers on First Fork Road can get to the river in two locations. The Sheep Creek Trail is 7 miles from the highway. From the well-marked trailhead, the trail drops 600 feet to the river in about a mile. At the river you can either fish downstream for about a mile to private land or fish upstream to the lower end of First Box Canyon. Remember that a strenuous climb back to your car awaits. A large flat river terrace with plenty of campsites is located where the trail meets the stream. Be aware that rattlesnakes are common along the lower Piedra up to First Fork Bridge.

Beyond Sheep Creek, Forest Road 622 ends at Piedra Bridge between First Box and Second Box Canyons. You can fish downstream from the bridge about a half-mile before reaching a difficult-to-wade stretch in the First Box Canyon. From the other side of the bridge the Piedra Trail parallels the river upstream for 12 miles to Forest Road 631. The trail usually remains within earshot of the river but makes a wide detour around Second Box Canyon. Many places along the trail offer easy access to the river. Campsites are not common, but wide benches on which one can pitch a tent occur near the river every half-mile or so. An overnight trip along the Piedra is a wild experience offering not only great fishing but the chance to see the river otters that live in the canyon.

The nearest lodging, restaurants, and groceries to the Piedra are found in Pagosa Springs. Closer to the river are the Forest Service's Bridge and Williams Creek Campgrounds along Forest Road 631. The campgrounds are on the banks of Williams Creek a few miles below Williams Creek Reservoir. Far downstream, near the river's crossing of U.S. 160, Lower Piedra Campground is located a mile from the highway on Forest Road 621. A primitive and often-crowded camping area is located at the end of First Fork Road at Piedra Bridge. To this undeveloped site take your own water and waste disposal materials.

The Piedra supports a large population of browns, rainbows, and cutbows, with many fish in the 12- to 14-inch class. On a good day fish seem to charge out from every lie to take flies. Just up from the U.S. 160 bridge near Lower Piedra Campground stocked rainbows dominate, but most trout in the long central valley are wild fish. Deep pools hold difficult-to-fool browns. Most of the rainbows are wild, strong, hard-fighting fish; the browns are wily fighters who often jump and who use rocks and currents to help them do their best to snap leaders.

As if to keep the Piedra from being too good to be true, the river exhibits one annoying characteristic. From the wilderness boundary down, the entire river can easily go off-color. The problem lies with the rocks underlying a few of the small tributary streams, and the prevalence of dirt roads in the middle of the watershed brings additional silt to the system. Murky runoff is to be expected, but summer storms along the

Piedra Valley or along any of its many tributaries can dirty the river. This is a common occurrence during July and August. Although the water often clears quickly, a couple of hours of cloudy flow can put fish down all day.

The upper forks of the Piedra offer miles of virtually untouched trout streams. Both the East and Middle Forks head well within the Weminuche Wilderness and offer miles of trailless, difficult-access fly fishing for brook trout and cutthroats. Downstream from the wilderness area the East Fork flows mainly through private land, but the Middle Fork offers 5 miles of excellent water within a half-mile of Forest Road 636. The stream and road come together about 1 mile north of the junction with Forest Road 637. From that point to the Middle Fork Trailhead the river flows just east of the road, and it is only a short walk to reach the water.

Out of the wilderness and beyond the mountain front the Middle Fork runs on an outwash plain through a wide canyon. From the river, one is almost always in sight of the volcanic peaks that form the striking backdrop. Elk are plentiful along the river in the morning and evening. It is a scenic river of startling beauty.

The Middle Fork flows over a cobble bottom with a braided channel. It is freestone water with long riffles, some deep runs, and a few pools. Willows and alders grow along the banks, but casting is free from obstructions within the stream channel. Wading is usually no problem. Rainbow and brown trout are the mainstay of the river.

Insect life is plentiful on the Middle Fork. Golden stones and small yellow sallies (stoneflies) hatch throughout the early summer. Size 8 to 12 Stimulators and size 14 or 16 Grizzly Wulffs are effective patterns at this time. Green drake hatches occur sporadically in mid- to late July and are easily matched with a Green Wulff in sizes 10 or 12. Pale morning duns are also on the water into August, and size 14 or 16 Light Cahills or yellow Humpys will match the naturals. Multiple mayfly hatches often occur at midday in July, when dry-fly fishing is

The pocket water on the Middle Fork of the Piedra River supports a large population of stoneflies, and patient anglers who cast stonefly nymphs into every possible lie will find plenty of trout. (Photograph by June Fabryka-Martin.)

at its peak. Anglers can choose either size 12 to 16 ginger, tan, or gray standard mayfly patterns or fish small attractor drys. Caddis provide afternoon action throughout the summer.

The East and Middle Forks join amid the rolling grasslands north of Pagosa Springs, and just below the confluence the main Piedra River enters a narrow valley. The river flows at the foot of Devil Mountain through sedimentary rocks turned nearly on end. Walking through the valley is easy most of the way, as is access to the stream. However, the sedimentary layers are broken by faults that bring ancient hard granite to the surface. The faults create two box canyons, not too creatively named First and Second Box Canyons as encountered by those heading upstream. Access to these rugged double canyons is difficult, and wading through them, when it is possible, requires extreme caution.

The long canyon at the base of Devil Mountain is the most important section of the river. For solitude, exquisite scenery, and a multitude of trout, this section of the Piedra is a sure bet. Heavy pressure is found near the roads on either end, but few anglers make the trip below the confluence with Williams Creek or walk as far as the box canyons. This entire stretch of the Piedra is managed as fly-and-lure only water. A two-fish limit is in effect throughout the stretch.

Because the Piedra in this stretch is hike-in water, four-piece 8½- to 9-foot rods are well suited for angling here. Midweight fly lines, from 4- to 6-weight, will help maintain control in the broken currents. Plan on rigging your rod with leaders from 7 to 9 feet long, and bring spools of stout 3X to 5X tippet. Wet wading won't turn you blue in July and August, but bring a pair of lightweight hip waders for comfortable fall fishing.

Near the Forest Road 631 bridge the stream is twenty to thirty feet wide with riffles, deep runs, and an abundance of pockets. The banks are open and clear of vegetation, and casting is easy almost everywhere. There are few deep holes to interfere with wading, but the rocks are slippery. A few hundred yards below the Forest Road 631 bridge, on land acquired by the Forest Service in the early 1990s, the river plunges into an interesting stretch of water flowing beneath overhanging cliffs.

The stream has a classic riffle-run-pool structure. Long sections hold smooth runs that are seemingly featureless, but don't ignore them. The piled cobbles on the river bottom offer protection for surprisingly large fish. Look for the deeper channels in the runs—any time the water is more than eighteen inches deep, a fish will be hiding in the gravel.

Farther downstream, beyond the confluence with Williams Creek, the river is about thirty feet across, widening to forty feet in the middle of the reach. The river cuts a straightforward course through the valley. The bottom is composed of slick, rounded cobbles. Casting from the stream is easy and virtually obstruction-free. Under normal flow conditions it is easy to cross the river in many spots. In the box canyons plunging pocket water, waterfalls, and streamside cliffs are the rule. Anglers who venture into these areas will find that getting around is very difficult if not impossible.

A large population of stoneflies is found in the Piedra, especially in and below the Second Box. Both *Pteronarcys* and *Hesperoperla* are found in the swift water. The salmon fly hatch usually coincides with heavy runoff in mid-June, when access and floating a dry fly are difficult. Following winters with low snowpack, dry-fly fishing this hatch can be exciting. Traditional patterns like Sofa Pillows or Bird's Stones along with large Elk Hair Caddis are effective in sizes 4 to 10. Cast to rising fish or make a hard cast that splashes the pattern into the water, then skim the fly across the surface. Hold on tight: A 14-inch rainbow in heavy currents can put up quite a fight.

During the hatch and throughout the rest of the year, stonefly nymphs are an excellent pattern choice on the river. Any favorite nymph pattern will do: a Giant Black Stone, Brooks Stone, or Bitch Creek Nymph. In pocket water and in runs along the cliffs, patterns can be fished with or without weight. When casting a nymph into the deepest pools, home to some big browns, getting a fly to the bottom is important. Cast to the heads and tails of the pools and in deep runs along the cliffs. For quick sinking, use a weighted pattern and add a bit of weight to the leader. If you are not getting strikes, add some weight until you feel the fly bouncing along or hanging up on the bottom.

Although the stream is known as stonefly water, sporadic mayfly hatches occur throughout the day in summer, and caddis are occasionally seen in the afternoon. High-floating, high-visibility attractor flies work well in midsummer. The House and Lot, Humpy, Renegade, and Parachute Adams are some local favorites to try. Float them with patience over all likely water. A trout can always be found lying in water over eighteen inches deep. Look for channels, pockets, and deep spots between boulders. Fish often strike hard when coming up a long way from deep lies. Grasshoppers are abundant along the river in late summer, and fly fishermen should take advantage of the presence of these terrestrials by casting big hopper patterns in the early afternoon.

Walking for miles to reach secluded stretches of river is not for every angler. The less adventurous can experience the Piedra near Lower Piedra Campground. Public water stretches about a mile below and a half-mile above the campground. The freestone and pocket water is similar to that found in the more remote sections of the river, and it holds plenty of rainbows in the 8- to 11-inch range. The banks are brush-lined, but casting can be done from just off the bank with little wading. This is a nice spot for beginners. Attractor drys and nymphs are all you need for a couple of hours of fun, particularly in the evening when the canyon is in shadow.

The Piedra offers some limited fishing opportunities on the Southern Ute Reservation. Below U.S. 160, the river drops below 6,500 feet and nears the edge of being a cold-water fishery. Trout are present but are more scattered than in the river above. The gradient flattens out and the river holds more riffles than pocket water. Cottonwoods line the banks as the river becomes more broad and shallow. Browns, rainbows, and Snake River cutthroats are found in this stretch.

Streamer fishing with sculpin minnow patterns can be very effective in this lower water. Fish the patterns right along the bottom where the trout, especially large browns, actively seek them out. Because the water temperatures are generally warm, the river fishes best early and late in the day. Also, the river is more prone to be off-color on the reservation. For details on sections of land open to public angling, consult the latest edition of the Southern Ute Indian Reservation Fishing Proclamation.

The Piedra River area is a wonderful place to spend a weekend. Over three dozen bird species live along the river, marmots hide in the rocks, and bear sign is common. With the abundance of trout and trout lies, one can fish all day and cover only a mile of stream. Start walking from any of the trailheads and force yourself to walk in a mile or two. It won't be easy to pass up the inviting stretches that you pass, but you can always fish them on the way out. You will rarely be disappointed by doing this.

WILLIAMS CREEK

Managed by: San Juan National Forest, Weminuche Wilderness
Access by: Vehicle and foot
Altitude: 7,500 to 10,500 feet
Type of Water: Rugged freestone stream
Best Times: Mid-June to October
Hatches: Mayflies, salmon flies, golden stones
Maps: USFS San Juan National Forest; USGS Cimarrona Peak and Oakbrush Ridge 7.5' quadrangles

---

Williams Creek is a major tributary of the Piedra River. The creek heads in the high country below Cimarrona Peak and flows through meadows and rugged canyons to be impounded in Williams Creek Reservoir just outside the wilderness boundary. Below the reservoir the creek flows through a 6-mile meadow before diving into a rocky canyon and joining the Piedra near the east end of its long valley section. The lower miles offer easy access by vehicle to fine fishing and grand scenery. The basin is surrounded by jagged 12,000-foot peaks, and the volcanic rock above timberline forms hulking domes, spires, and banded mountain masses of subtle beauty.

Williams Creek is reached via Piedra Road west of Pagosa Springs. From U.S. 160 about 2 miles west of the center of town, head north on Piedra Road. The paved road soon becomes all-weather gravel and remains suitable for all vehicles. The road, now identified as Forest Road 631, parallels

Williams Creek about 15 miles from U.S. 160. Bridge and Williams Creek Campgrounds offer a good base of operations for fishing the stream. The wilderness portion of Williams Creek is located beyond Williams Creek Reservoir, about 25 miles from Pagosa Springs.

In the Weminuche Wilderness, Williams Creek is wild and tumbling, flowing through rugged terrain. Trail 587, which begins at the Williams Creek Trailhead just above the reservoir, parallels the stream but is rarely alongside it. The canyon is rough—boulders, cliffs, swift water, narrow chutes filled with water—for 3.5 miles upstream from the Williams Creek Trailhead and is for strong, confident hiking anglers only. The stream is brushy and flows through deep conifer woods. Fish from the banks or plan to wade wet. Many small box canyons limit the angler's ability to walk along the stream, but good access is found off Trail 588, 3.5 miles from the trailhead. About 4 miles in, several small meadows open up some easier fishing opportunities. The best way to fish the upper creek is to backpack into the meadows, set up camp in the bordering timber, then fish the meadows and the canyon stretch below.

Not many trout are found in the wilderness portion of the stream. Look for them in slack water—along banks, behind boulders, in deep runs or pockets. Because of the clear water, use caution when approaching the stream, and keep a low profile. The wilderness is home to some heavy cutbows—slow and lazy fish that will sip a fly, then think about it for a moment before deciding to put up a fight. Anglers will find fish in the 12- to 15-inch range.

Below the wilderness and Williams Creek Reservoir, in the area of the Williams Creek and Bridge Campgrounds, the creek remains a fine trout stream. Rainbows are found throughout the stretch, and browns in the 12- to 15-inch range swim the deepest water. Here the creek is fifteen to twenty feet wide and up to four feet deep and is a freestone stream with runs and riffles and a few pools. Deep slicks are located in the bends, and some deep runs are found through

Williams Creek is small, but good-sized brown trout often lie in the deeper runs near the willows. (Photograph by Craig Martin.)

the willows. The bottom is composed of boulders and clean cobbles. Wading is easy in hip boots; wet wading will work just fine. Most of the banks are open, but willows create some narrow spots where casting is tight. Typical tackle for this water is a 7½- to 8½-foot rod, 3- or 4-weight line, and stout tippet.

Runoff ends and the water is clear by mid-June. Summer insects are abundant, especially when the water warms up a bit in the late afternoon. Midges, mayflies up to size 12, small yellow stoneflies, and some afternoon caddis are found here. Williams Creek is primarily a stonefly stream with a very abundant salmon fly population. The hatch usually occurs in mid-June during runoff when high water levels make fishing dry flies difficult. Stonefly and beadhead nymphs are effective not only during the hatch but throughout the year.

Williams Creek affords fine dry-fly fishing all summer. Larger flies—sizes 10 to 14—are best. A Parachute Adams will take fish all day; in late evening a Parachute Brown Wulff works well. Many trout lies are found within the rocks, along the banks, and in the deeper water. Larger fish hold in front and behind submerged boulders in deep runs. Cast to small pockets of slack water, which often hide good fish.

A seldom-fished stretch of Williams Creek lies in a narrow canyon below Ice Cave Ridge. This stretch is best reached from the Piedra River Trail beginning near the Piedra Bridge on Forest Road 631. Hike downstream along the Piedra about 1 mile to a footbridge that crosses Williams Creek. From here, fish upstream into the pocket water along Williams Creek. In contrast to the meadows above, this tumbling section of stream requires the use of high-floating drys and weighted nymphs. Again, stonefly nymphs are an excellent choice. Because these fish see few fishermen, attractor dry flies and terrestrials are adequate for most days on the river.

To
Hunchback Pass

Leviathan Cr.

Rock Creek

Flint
Lakes

To
Weminuche Pass

Sunlight
Peak

Rock
Lake

Granite
Lake

Johnson

Creek

Creek

Moon
Lake

Flint Creek

Divide
Lakes

To FR 631

Echo
Mountain

Lake

Emerald
Lake

Little
Emerald
Lake

Willow
Park

Falls   Creek

First Bridge

Vallecito

Wilderness

Creek

Los Pinos River

Granite
Peak

Vallecito

Pine
River

600

602

Weminuche

private

**Los Pinos River
and
Vallecito Creek**

Vallecito
Reservoir

603

N

To
Durango

501

0   4

8

THE LOS PINOS
AND FLORIDA WATERSHEDS

LOS PINOS RIVER (THE PINE)

Managed by: San Juan National Forest, Weminuche Wilderness, Southern Ute Reservation
Access by: Foot
Altitude: 6,200 to 10,500 feet
Type of Water: Freestone, pocket water, meadows
Best Times: Early July to late September
Hatches: Caddisflies, mayflies, blue-winged olives
Maps: USFS San Juan National Forest; USGS Granite Lake, Emerald Lake, Granite Peak, Vallecito Reservoir, Ludwig Mountain, Bayfield, and Tiffany 7.5' quadrangles

The southwestern half of the Weminuche Wilderness Area is drained by two major streams—the Los Pinos and Florida Rivers—and their tributaries. Of these, the Los Pinos watershed is the largest, covering a sprawling portion of the wilderness west of the Continental Divide. The Florida watershed is much smaller, draining a narrow glacial valley south of Columbine Pass.

The Los Pinos River is known locally as the Pine. The river is divided into two distinct sections by the extensive impoundment of Vallecito Reservoir. The southern portion of the river below the reservoir is completely on private land and the Southern Ute Reservation, and fishing opportunities are limited. Between the reservoir and the Weminuche Wilderness the Pine flows through about 6 miles of private land, but from the wilderness boundary to the Continental Divide the Pine offers backcountry fly fishing at its finest. With over 50 miles of stream amid exquisite scenery, the possibilities for fishing adventures in the Los Pinos watershed are nearly limitless.

The Pine lies far from any towns, but Vallecito Reservoir is the centerpiece of a large developed area that offers food, lodging, gas, and a wide variety of campgrounds. Other services are available in Durango, a short drive to the west. A small Forest Service campground is located at the Pine River Trailhead, and many other Forest Service campgrounds are found near the reservoir.

The trout found within the wilderness portion of the Pine watershed are exclusively wild fish. In the lower two-thirds of the river all common species of trout are found: rainbows, brookies, browns, and cutthroats. Above Willow Park mostly cutthroats and brook trout are found, along with an occasional rainbow. Below Flint Creek the average fish is around 8 to 10 inches. Trout up to 14 inches are common, with isolated larger fish. The entire watershed within the wilderness has special regulations. Angling is limited to flies and lures, and there is a bag and possession limit of two fish.

The upper Pine is entirely hike-in water. The easiest access to the river begins at the Pine River Trailhead east of Vallecito Reservoir at Granite Peak Ranch. The first 3 miles of river above the trailhead, as well as the trail itself, pass through the private ranch. No fishing is permitted on the ranch, and hikers into the wilderness must stay on the trail until reaching the national forest boundary. Day trips into the wilderness are possible as long as one doesn't mind the 6-mile round-trip walk.

The Pine River Trail #523 receives heavy use from backpackers and horsemen and from anglers heading to the Flint Lakes, Emerald Lake, and the upper Pine drainage. The wide trail has one of the most gentle climbs in the wilderness, which accounts for much of its popularity. In spite of such heavy use, it is still possible to find solitude amid the mountain scenery along the Pine. The remote river canyon invites overnight trips and extended stays in the backcountry. Trips up the valley of the Pine can range from 6 to 40 miles, attracting backpackers of all abilities, even young children.

Backpacking with a fly rod is one of the supreme pleasures of angling in the San Juan Mountains. Those setting out for an overnight stay in the wilderness should travel prepared to meet the mountains on their own terms. Sturdy hiking boots, foul-weather gear, and extra layers of warm clothing are essential, as is a tent for protection from the almost daily summer rains. To keep impact on the fragile wilderness landscape to a minimum, use only well-established campsites and cook with a fuel-operated stove. Four-piece travel rods are easy to lash onto backpacks, eliminating the need to carry a rod in-hand for a long distance. Bring a small hip pack or fisherman's lanyard to organize and hold your angling gear when the hiking is over and the fishing begins. A small fly box with a carefully selected collection of flies rounds out the necessary equipment for a successful trip.

To reach the Pine River Trailhead from Bayfield, go north from U.S. 160 on Vallecito Road, County Road 501. In about 8 miles bear right, then continue straight at the junction with County Road 240. This point can be reached from Durango by taking Florida Road (County Road 240) about 17 miles from the north part of town. Reach Vallecito Dam in another 9 miles and continue on County Road 501 along the west bank of the reservoir. At the Forest Service Vallecito Work Center, bear right onto Forest Road 602 and continue around the lake and up the Pine River about 7.5 miles to the trailhead at Pine River Campground.

Begin the hike into the scenic granite canyon of the Pine

and the public water above Granite Peak Ranch by following the Pine River Trail as it heads east parallel to a fence. Off to the right of the trail the river looks tantalizing: However, do not trespass. Stay on the trail until reaching the wilderness boundary, 3 miles from the start. In the wilderness, fine fly fishing is found everywhere on the river.

Above the wilderness boundary the Pine flows through a broad flat-bottomed canyon overlooked by sheer walls of blocky granite. With most anglers headed to more remote destinations, the stretch of river just above the wilderness boundary is well worth the effort for those looking for a day trip. Much of the river in the first 2 miles of public water is relatively open with easy casting, easy wading, and plenty of small brook trout and browns. Most trout are small, but a few nice fish up to 16 inches can be found.

This lower stretch of the Pine is an ideal place for beginning fly fishermen and children. The open nature of the riverbanks, the slow pace of the river currents, and the plentiful brook trout melt away many of the frustrations that beginners often face. Little wading is required, and casting from the gravel bars into the main flow or to the deeper runs near the opposite bank is an easy technique that can quickly lead to a fish. Pattern selection is unimportant, and beginners can fish easily seen white-winged attractors or grasshopper patterns with good results. To make fishing as easy as possible, those just starting out in the sport can fish House and Lot, Royal Trude, Royal Wulff, and parachute hopper patterns tied with a white post.

Beyond the intersection with the Emerald Lake Trail, about 6 miles from the start, the Pine flows through a thundering canyon. Boulders, plunge pools, and waterfalls are found for the next 3 miles. Here anglers must scramble down from the trail to reach the river below. Frequently the canyon bottom is boxed in, so expect to work hard to fish this stretch of water. Anglers will find fewer fishermen in this stretch than in the more popular water above. It is not uncommon for the banks to be brushy in this stretch, and casting can be difficult. The stream is up to forty feet wide, but it can't be crossed everywhere. Most casts can be made from the banks, and wading is not always necessary. If you get into the water, hip boots with good felt soles will be useful. The bottom is slick and the currents are fast.

Scattered pools up to eight feet deep and thousands of pockets make this stretch worth the effort. A quarter-mile of stream should keep you busy the entire afternoon. With either high-floating dry flies or nymphs, use a short leader. The turbulent water permits getting up close to the fish, and memorable fish can be taken from a rod's length away. To get a more natural float through the complicated currents, keep most of the fly line off the water. Use short-line nymphing techniques to get subsurface patterns to the bottom of the river.

In fast currents trout don't have time to think much about food floating by, and so the fish in the pocket water are not very fussy. Use high-floating patterns designed for rough water. Select a Humpy, any of the Wulff series, or an Irresistible. Large sizes, from 10 to 14, are effective. Apply a generous coat of floatant to the fly. Cast into all small pockets of slack water along the stream edges, behind and in front of rocks, and at the foot of plunge pools. It takes only a couple of seconds of good drift to induce a strike. Keeping most of the fly line off the water will help get a drag-free float through the complex currents.

Nymphs can also be effective in the pocket water. In the fast currents patterns should be large and have a bit of flash. Any pattern with peacock can be effective, for instance a Zug Bug or Prince Nymph. More subtle nymphs, like the Gold-Ribbed Hare's Ear, Muskrat, March Brown, and Pheasant Tail, work well in sizes 10 to 14.

Above the canyon about 9 miles from the trailhead the valley opens up into the lovely Willow Park. Here the river meanders through long open meadows in a scenic valley with

Holding your rod high will help you get a drag-free drift in the pocket water on the Los Pinos River below Willow Park. (Photograph by June Fabryka-Martin.)

waterfalls cascading down the cliffs on the east side. It is a wonderful spot in which to spend a couple of days. Carry in a four-piece travel rod at least 8 feet long, and some 9-foot leaders and 4X to 5X tippet material.

At Willow Park the Pine is still a small river from thirty to forty feet wide. Anglers will find a twisting stream with dozens of turns. The river is typical meadow water with shallow gravel bars, meanders, and deep undercut banks. Riffles are common, as are smooth-running slicks and stillwater bends. Few rocks break the surface of the water. The banks are mostly free from obstructions, and casting is easy from almost everywhere. The bottom is clean gravel, and wading is easy. In summer, plan on wet wading in old running shoes or all-terrain sandals.

The trout in the meadow water are wilderness fish, but

they are not as fussy as one might think. However, because this area receives moderate use from anglers, the trout are spooky: A careful approach to the stream is required. Stay low, and keep casting to a minimum. Any fly line drifting over a fish will put it down, so carefully plan each cast to insure that only the tippet will float near the target. Wade as little as possible, but crisscrossing the stream to get into the best casting position is important.

Dry flies are an exciting way to fool the trout in the Willow Park area. Cast to rising fish, or prospect with attractors through the riffles. Pay special attention to the numerous undercut banks found in the turns of the stream. A dead-drift float is almost always appropriate. Throughout the summer evening caddis is the most important hatch of the day. Sporadic mayfly hatches do occur, and anglers should try to match major bug events. Most important are attractor patterns. In still water or during thin mayfly hatches, Parachute Adams, Ginger Duns, or yellow-bodied Comparaduns in sizes 14 or 16 are excellent. A pattern that has proven its worth on many occasions is the House and Lot size 14. In the late afternoon and evening a Peacock Caddis in size 12 or 14 is the best bet. In late summer and fall a blue-winged olive hatch is important.

In the mountain meadows of the Pine and other streams in the San Juans, anglers should always consider terrestrials as important patterns. In general, streams become relatively nutrient-poor as one nears the headwaters. This limits the number of aquatic insects found in the water and emphasizes the importance of terrestrial insects that fall, fly, or are blown into the water from overhanging vegetation. In the summer months grasshoppers, beetles, and ants are an excellent all-around first choice of pattern. Dave's Hoppers, Parachute Hoppers, or Dry Muddlers are effective throughout hopper season. In early summer patterns can be up to size 6, but in the fall keep the imitations no larger than size 10. To imitate smaller terrestrials, foam beetles and dubbed or foam ants are good choices.

Mimic the action of natural insects as closely as possible. Ants and beetles normally float dead-drift on the currents, at times floating on the surface and at other times moving below the surface. Rubber legs on beetle patterns often add a bit of motion to the pattern that reflects the moving legs of the natural. Grasshoppers can be floated on the surface or drifted as wet flies just beneath the film.

About 2 miles above the upper end of Willow Park the river divides into Flint Creek and the main branch of the Pine. From here to the headwaters both streams are creek size, much smaller than below in Willow Park. Good trails parallel both streams. The left branch of the trail leads to the Flint Lakes, which are about 6 miles from and 2,000 feet higher than the confluence. The Pine continues 10 miles northeast to Weminuche Pass on the Continental Divide. On both creeks stream gradients are higher than on the Pine below, and the trails that parallel the streams are correspondingly steeper. Fewer hikers and anglers are encountered in the upper reaches of each stream.

Above Flint Creek the Pine is about 10 feet wide; Flint Creek is a bit smaller. On the Pine, an impressive falls is located within a half-mile of the Flint Creek Trail junction. Both streams alternate between meadow and pocket water. Cutthroats and some rainbows ranging from 6 to 10 inches are found in the upper waters. As with most high-altitude trout, the fish are spooky but not selective in their feeding habits. Fish with attractor drys and terrestrials, using the careful tactics required by skittish trout.

The Flint Lakes lie at the head of Flint Creek about 16 miles from the trailhead. Nearby are Moon Lake and Rock Lake, beautiful cirque lakes tucked up against the peaks. Across the main branch of the Pine, Granite and Divide Lakes offer quality high-elevation-lake fishing. This section of the Weminuche Wilderness holds more high-elevation lakes than one could fish in a lifetime. Wanderers along the Continental Divide can use topographic maps to spot additional interesting lakes to try.

Most of the lakes in the area hold good populations of cutthroat, rainbow, and brook trout. *Callibaetis* mayflies, some caddisflies, and midges are the mainstays of these lakes. Dry flies can be effective in the midday *Callibaetis* hatch and in the evening when midges and some caddis are on the water. Actively fishing subsurface patterns is the best technique the rest of the day. Try casting caddis pupae, midge pupae, and streamers.

Granite Lake and the upper reaches of the Pine can be reached via a shorter hike beginning at the Poison Park Trailhead located near Williams Lake out of Pagosa Springs. Trails 592 and 539 lead to the upper Pine about 5 miles above Flint Creek. The trip is about 10 miles one way.

Snow generally limits access to the Pine throughout runoff, which begins in late April. High water continues through mid-June, or later during years following high winter snowpack. Conditions are perfect from July through September. Fall trips on the Pine are delightful, with red oaks and yellow willows adding a splash of color to the cliffs. Anglers will encounter fewer people on the river after Labor Day.

Those seeking less of a wilderness experience should consider the possibilities of Vallecito Reservoir, where water from the Pine and Vallecito Creek is impounded. Aside from easy access, the main attraction of the lake is the large fish that swim in its water. Rainbow and brown trout as well as northern pike grow to monstrous proportions in the fertile water.

The reservoir presents a challenge to the fly fisherman. It is intimidating to fish from a float tube, but fly fishing from a power boat is possible. Float-tubing is best in the upper end of both arms of the reservoir, where there is some shelter from the wind. The inlet areas also offer a small forest of partially and completely submerged stumps that provide excellent cover for brown trout and northern pike. Browns hold in this area all year, but mid-May through mid-June is best for pike. The reservoir offers a good opportunity to fish in late spring, when the rivers in the area are high with runoff.

For each of us, the Los Pinos River holds special memories of angling trips with friends and family. The easy grades of the walk into the wilderness and the open nature of the valleys endlessly beckon us in our dreams, both at night and during the day. Even without the speckled and spotted wild trout found in the rolling currents, the Pine canyon would be a special place amid a region filled with exquisite beauty.

EMERALD LAKES
AND LAKE CREEK

Managed by: San Juan National Forest, Weminuche Wilderness
Access by: Foot or horseback
Altitude: 10,033 feet
Type of Water: Large and small natural lakes, pocket water
Best Times: Late June to September
Hatches: Midges, *Callibaetis*
Maps: USFS San Juan National Forest; USGS Emerald Lake 7.5' quadrangle

The Pine River drainage is dotted with an abundance of high-altitude lakes found along trails deep in the Weminuche Wilderness. Two popular ones, Emerald and Little Emerald Lakes, are located along Lake Creek, a major tributary of the Pine River. For those who hike or ride a horse up from the Pine River Trailhead, these lakes offer excellent angling for trout in a beautiful setting. On the route to the lakes, Lake Creek traverses some rugged terrain as it provides the opportunity to fish for a variety of trout in wild pocket water.

Emerald Lake, the third largest natural lake in Colorado, held no fish until cutthroat trout from the Pine River were stocked there in 1888. Later a private fish hatchery was built on the lakeshore, and rainbows from this source were also stocked in the lake. When the hatchery was abandoned, the brood stock of rainbows was let loose into the lake, creating a strong population of wild cutthroat-rainbow hybrids that remain in the lake today. Cutbow hybrids from Emerald Lake are used as genetic stock for plantings in other high-mountain lakes in Colorado.

To protect this unique fishery, Colorado Division of Wildlife manages the lake as wild trout water. Angling is limited to flies and artificial lures only. There is a two-fish bag and possession limit, and the fish must be under 14 inches. To protect spawning fish, angling is prohibited at the inlet and upstream in Lake Creek a half-mile above the inlet from January 1 to July 15.

It takes a bit of work to get to the Emerald Lakes, but this doesn't discourage many anglers, and the lake is a popular spot for fishermen. Anglers can make the long hike into the lake with backpacks, use horses, or hire one of the many outfitters that pack in visitors and their gear. Access to the lakes is by 10 miles of trail beginning at the Pine River Trailhead. The first 3 miles of the popular Pine River Trail pass through the private Granite Peak Ranch. The trail climbs gently 6 miles to the junction with the Emerald Lake Trail. Turn left onto the Emerald Lake Trail, which immediately begins to climb steeply up the canyon of Lake Creek. In the 4 miles to the lake the trail climbs 1,500 feet. Numerous avalanche chutes along the route can be covered with snow until late July.

Because of the popularity of the area, camping restrictions are in effect along the lake. No camping is permitted within one-quarter mile south of the lake and within a half-mile north, west, and east of the lake. These regulations will help return this heavily used area to a more natural state.

To reach the trailhead from Bayfield, go north from U.S. 160 on Vallecito Road, County Road 501. In about 8 miles bear right, then go straight at the junction with County Road 240. This point can be reached from Durango by taking Florida Road (County Road 240) about 17 miles from the north part of town. Reach Vallecito Dam in another 9 miles and continue on County Road 501 along the west bank of the reservoir. At the Forest Service Vallecito Work Center, bear right onto Forest Road 602 and continue around the lake and up the Pine River about 7.5 miles to the trailhead at Pine River Campground.

Between the Pine River and Little Emerald Lake, Lake Creek offers rugged, challenging fishing in churning pocket water. The stream provides a fine excuse for taking a rest on the long hike in to the lakes. Give yourself an hour or two and get in a bit of angling. Plenty of fish are found throughout the stream, with brown, brook, rainbow, and cutthroat trout all present. The stream is brush-lined and difficult to fish. High-floating flies and a lot of patience are required for this stretch. Above the lakes, Lake Creek holds brook trout and cutbow hybrids all the way up to Moon Lake. It is a fine little stream and much easier to fish than in the rugged canyon below the lake.

Emerald Lake has a surface area of 280 acres, and Little Emerald Lake is 15 acres. Both lakes are clean and free of weeds. It is easy to find places to make obstruction-free casts along the bank. The lakes are good for float tubes, if you can carry one up the long trail. Trout often congregate near the inlet and to a lesser extent at the outlet. The water can be cold, and anglers who plan to spend a lot of time standing in the water would do well to bring along a pair of hip waders. You will need to make long casts when fishing this and other high-country lakes, so bring a 9-foot rod and 5- or 6-weight line.

At 10,033 feet Emerald Lake is not a timberline lake and thus is more fertile than most other high-country lakes in the Weminuche Wilderness. Aquatic insects are common, but the fish are characteristically opportunistic feeders. In general, the fish in the lake will take a look at anything that resembles an insect or forage fish that comes their way. Take advantage of this trait by using Woolly Buggers and terrestrials as searching patterns. Also very effective are black, brown, and winged ant patterns in sizes 14 to 18. Ants can be effectively fished along the shore and under overhanging vegetation. Small beetle patterns with a bit of added flash on the body also work well along the banks. When no trout are rising, fishing nymphs at the inlet is a good technique to use. Cast into the current and allow the nymph to swing into the lake. Bucktail streamers imitate small trout and can bring some interest from the larger fish in the lake.

Many hatches occur on the lake, and anglers should come prepared to match them. Big caddisflies are found on the water in late afternoon throughout the summer. Adult caddis patterns such as Peacock Caddis or Colorado King in sizes 10 or 12 can be successful, but emerging caddis larvae patterns can work magic. Try a Tellico Nymph or any color partridge soft-hackle in sizes 12 to 16. Gary LaFontaine's emerging caddis pupa patterns in rust and yellow are another fine choice. When fishing caddis pupa in still water, let the pattern sink before pulling it toward the surface with a series of short strips. Patience pays when angling for cruising trout in big water.

Speckle-winged mayflies of the genus *Callibaetis* hatch throughout the summer. The hatches can occur at any time of day but are most numerous midmorning or on cloudy days. Fish a size 14 or 16 Parachute Adams or, better yet, an old-fashioned Light Cahill tied parachute-style. When fishing these patterns to rising trout, be sure to have at least 10 feet of leader ending with a length of 5X or 6X tippet. Make a soft cast four to six feet in front of cruising trout. Light-bodied nymph patterns such as a Gold-Ribbed Hare's Ear or a Timberline in size 14 or 16 are also effective during this hatch.

In summer, damselflies are abundant on the Emerald Lakes. Dry blue damselfly patterns in sizes 8 to 12 are excellent imitations for the local species. When fishing damselfly drys (or almost any other dry fly) on a lake, watch for rising trout and note the fish's riseform. Try to anticipate the fish's next move. Cast one or two feet in front of where you esti-mate the fish will rise again, and get ready for the slurp. If the trout misses the fly, carefully retrieve the line from the surface and cast again.

Olive damselfly nymphs imitate the abundant immature in-sects found in the Emerald Lakes. Select a pattern that ex-hibits plenty of movement, such as one with lots of marabou in the tail and gill areas. Lake fishing with nymphs is best with a weighted pattern or a small amount of weight on the leader above the nymph. Look for some kind of subsurface struc-ture—submerged logs or stumps, rocks, or ledges. Cast to the structure and let the nymph sink. Mimic the natural swimming motion of the insect by lifting the fly two to three feet with the rod tip, then letting it sink again. Retrieve the slack line cre-ated by this motion, then repeat the process until you reach the end of the line or a trout grabs your pattern on the run.

When midges swarm above the water in the evening, midge pupa and adult patterns are effective. Bring a selection of colors—black, gray, tan, and olive—and try them all until you find the color that works best at the particular time. Fish midge pupa patterns just below the surface using a greased leader. Apply floatant to the leader up to a point a couple inches from the fly. This will keep the leader and tippet on top while the pupa is suspended a couple of inches below the sur-face film. If midges fail to do the trick in the evening, try strip-ping a Woolly Bugger at varying depths.

VALLECITO CREEK

Managed by: Private, San Juan National Forest, Weminuche
   Wilderness
Access by: Foot
Altitude:7,600 to 12,300 feet

Type of Water: Freestone, pocket water, meadows
Best Times: Early July to mid-September
Hatches: Mayflies, midges
Maps: USFS San Juan National Forest: USGS Vallecito Reservoir, Columbine Pass, and Storm King 7.5' quadrangles

---

A serious angler could fish forever along Vallecito Creek, popping flies into the creek's thousands of inviting riffles and pools, learning the secrets of a 20-mile stretch of fascinating high-country water. The not-so-serious can simply delight in the stream's clear water as it tumbles over falls and slows into pools ten feet deep, allowing sight of every pebble on the bottom. The scenic quality of the canyon, the majesty of the surrounding mountains, and the beauty of the stream itself are unmatched in the San Juan Mountains.

Vallecito Creek is a long but small stream located almost entirely within the Weminuche Wilderness. Its public stretch is accessible only by foot along well-used trails. The spectacular scenery of the Vallecito area is well known, and the lower miles of the trails along the creek receive heavy use by day hikers, backpackers, and fishermen. With plenty of room to spread out, the Vallecito Valley never seems crowded. A half-dozen major tributary streams add to the attraction of the watershed. Opportunities to spend a week of wilderness fishing are endless. An outstanding weeklong trip is to hike up the Vallecito and Rock Creeks to the Flint Lakes, then descend along Flint Creek and the Los Pinos River. Fly-fishing nirvana!

The trailhead for the Vallecito Creek Trail is located above Vallecito Reservoir. From Durango, take Florida Road, County Road 240, north and west from 15th Street for 17 miles to the intersection with County Road 501 and turn left. (This point can also be reached 8.5 miles from Bayfield north on County Road 501.) Continue on County Road 501 about 9.5 miles past Vallecito Dam and Reservoir. Just beyond the Forest Service Vallecito Work Center, bear left on Forest Road

600 and continue about 3 miles through Vallecito Campground to the trailhead for the Vallecito Trail. The trail follows the creek about 16 miles before leaving the valley floor to climb Hunchback Pass.

Gas, food, and lodging are available on the roads along Vallecito Reservoir. Additional services are available in Durango. Private campgrounds are found along the lake, and plenty of sites are found at the Forest Service's Vallecito Campground at the end of Forest Road 600.

Although it is primarily a backpacker's paradise, several options are available for day hikes on the Vallecito Trail. From the trailhead, hike up the trail as it climbs steeply away from the river to skirt a narrow rocky gorge along the stream. After about 1.5 miles the trail descends to creek level for a few hundred yards. Here you will find some excellent pocket water. Those with more time and energy can continue hiking upstream to a string of small meadows above the first footbridge over the creek, making a 6-mile round-trip.

To explore the long middle and upper sections of the Vallecito, plan on at least one night in the wilderness. Camping locations are found between the two footbridges on the lower 5 miles of stream and in the extensive meadows above Dead Horse Creek, 7 miles from the trailhead.

Vallecito is creek-sized from the headwaters to the reservoir. The stream ranges from six feet in width in the upper reaches to ten feet wide in the meadows to more than twenty feet wide in the lower canyon section. It has a clean rocky bottom throughout. The water is almost always crystal clear, which, combined with the pastel colors of the streambed rocks, makes for a stream as pretty as any in Colorado.

The sprawling watershed has much terrain above timberline, which creates an extended runoff. High water begins in late April and continues through late June or early July. Although the stream is fishable during runoff, dangerous currents make fishing then unadvisable. The stream is in its prime from mid-July to mid-September.

Even if the trout refuse to take all your offerings, angling the crystal-clear water of Vallecito Creek is always a delight. (Photograph by June Fabryka-Martin.)

Wild rainbow, cutthroat, and brook trout are found in Vallecito Creek. The fish are appropriate for the size of the stream, generally in the 8- to 12-inch range. Some deeper water in the Vallecito and its tributaries holds fine trout up to 16 inches, but these are the exceptions. The entire Vallecito within the Weminuche Wilderness is managed as fly-and-lure-only water, and there is a bag and possession limit of two fish in effect. Anglers within the wilderness are encouraged to limit their catch and to release all fish over 12 inches back to the water.

About a half-mile above the trailhead the Vallecito flows wildly through a narrow gorge with a high stream gradient. This stretch has the most difficult access of any part of the creek. Large boulders and tight vegetation make this an awkward place to fly fish. The stream plunges over waterfalls and through pocket water for about 2 miles. Most of the trout in this section of river are small, but difficult-to-reach pools often hold larger trout. Wear hip boots and plan to stay out of the stream as much as possible. Always use caution when fishing this stretch.

Because the stream is small and the vegetation is thick there, a short rod is best for fly fishing the gorge of the Vallecito. Use 8-foot leaders and stout tippet, and plan on keeping most of the fly line off the water. Most casts can be made by flipping the end of the rod, or just reach and place the fly in the desired current. Work many short casts into every possible trout lie on the way upstream. Either wet or dry flies can be effective in the pocket water.

Fly fishing is less taxing past the first footbridge on the Vallecito Trail and upstream in the wide valley at the foot of the Needle Mountains. Here the stream flows through more open country, and wading and casting are easier than below. The Vallecito still has a high gradient, but intermittent meadows offer twists, bends, and undercut banks. Stealth tactics need not be so rigorous as on more quiet waters. To avoid spooking larger fish, keep wading and casting to a minimum. Be prepared to fish the water thoroughly, casting to every likely lie in the stream. Patience will be amply rewarded.

Vallecito Creek has a wide variety of aquatic and terrestrial insects. Mayfly hatches occur throughout the summer, and caddisflies swarm over the river in the evening. When bugs are on the water, almost any fly pattern can be successful. Use an Adams, an old reliable Blue Dun, an Elk Hair Caddis, a Royal Wulff, or a Renegade in sizes 14 to 18 in the quieter stretches. Watch for red quills in late July, and fish the hatch with a size 12 to 14 Red Quill pattern. In July a fine hatch of golden stoneflies occurs along the entire creek. During the hatch, dry-fly fishing with a size 10 Stimulator can be exciting, or try skittering a size 10 Dry Muddler across the surface. Stonefly nymphs are an excellent choice at any time. Winged wet flies and soft-hackles are excellent searching patterns. Swing wet flies through pools and pockets, being careful not to disturb the surface with the fly.

For most of the summer, terrestrials are the most important insects on the water. The abundance of overhanging vegetation and the wide meadows lining the stream bring a wide variety of ants, beetles, and grasshoppers into the water. Black and brown ant patterns are a fine choice to fish along the banks in quiet water. Under trees and willows, beetles from size 10 to 16 will often bring a trout to the surface. In the meadows, hoppers are found in a wide range of sizes from 8 to 14. Fish them with a hard cast to make a splash, then pull them in a series of short twitches across the surface.

As you climb up the valley on the Vallecito Trail, the creek becomes smaller as major tributaries enter. The first major branch is Johnson Creek, about 8.5 miles from the trailhead. Fishg is good on this tributary, but the area is often crowded with hikers coming down from Columbine Pass. Above Roell Creek, a mineral seep located on a slope above Rock Creek adversely affects the water quality in the Vallecito. Angling in this stretch is generally poor, with only a few small brook trout and cutbow hybrids present. Conditions improve above the junction with Rock Creek, but at this elevation the Vallecito is rather small.

Grab a four-piece rod and a backpack and head up the Vallecito. If you can keep your mind off the exquisite scenery for a few minutes, you'll find plenty of trout willing to sample your flies.

FLORIDA RIVER

Managed by: San Juan National Forest, Weminuche Wilderness, private
Access by: Vehicle and foot
Altitude: 6,300 to 12,500 feet
Type of Water: Freestone, pocket water, meadows
Best Times: Early July through September
Hatches: Caddisflies, mayflies, stoneflies
Maps: USFS San Juan National Forest; USGS Columbine Pass, Mountain View Crest, and Lemon Reservoir 7.5' quadrangles

*F*lorida is a Spanish word, pronounced *flow-REE-da*, meaning "lush" or "flowery." The valley of the Florida River is indeed verdant as the river flows out of the San Juan Mountains to the Animas River. Like the Los Pinos River just to the east, the Florida is divided into two sections by a reservoir, in this case Lemon Reservoir. Below the dam the river is entirely private and anglers must have permission to fish. Some public water is found in the miles above the reservoir, but the best fishing on the stream is in the Weminuche Wilderness. Unlike the Pine, access to the Florida in the wilderness is difficult at best. Angling the Florida is for the most adventurous of fly fishermen.

Access to all parts of the Florida watershed is via County Road 243 along Lemon Reservoir. From Durango, take

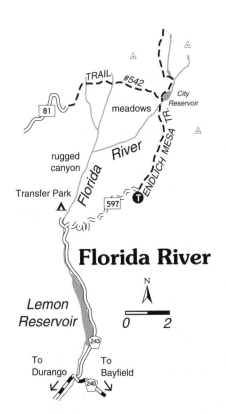

Florida Road, County Road 240, north and east from town about 14 miles to County Road 243. From Bayfield, reach County Road 243 by driving about 8.5 miles north on Vallecito Road, County Road 501, to the intersection with County Road 240. Turn left and continue about 3 miles to County Road 243. Turn north toward Lemon Dam and continue to the intersection with Forest Road 597. Here the road parallels the river. Continue straight about 2 miles to Transfer Park Campground.

Lemon Reservoir is smaller and less developed than nearby Vallecito Reservoir. Lemon Reservoir can be fly fished from the banks, from pontoons, or from small boats. Rainbows are the most common trout in the reservoir, and some are over 20 inches. Most attractive to anglers is the presence in spring and early summer of very large brown trout. Midges and forage fish are the most important food sources. Fish all day with streamers, or in the evening switch to midge patterns. The best fishing is found near the inlet of the Florida and at the inlets of small streams draining into the impoundment.

Anglers will find that the Florida holds plenty of small trout in an assortment of species. Between Lemon and City Reservoirs brown, brook, cutbow, and rainbow trout are found. Most of these wild fish are in the 6- to 10-inch range, with isolated larger trout in the more difficult to reach pools. Above City Reservoir brown trout drop out and are replaced by cutthroats. The fish in the upper stretches of the Florida are all small. No special regulations are in effect throughout the watershed.

Above Lemon Reservoir the Florida flows through 2 miles of private land. Public water is found between Florida and Transfer Park Campgrounds. With easy access along a gravel road this stretch of the river is fished hard and is best left to the bait fishermen.

Access to the Florida from the end of Forest Road 597 presents the angler with a challenge. Trail 667 begins at Transfer Park Campground and heads north into the wilderness but never comes close to the river. No trail parallels the river from Transfer Park to City Reservoir. The first 2 miles of the river canyon above Transfer Park are very rugged. To try your luck on this section of river you must fight through vegetation and rocks to work upstream. Those who bushwhack into this rugged area will be rewarded for their efforts with spectacular waterfalls, deep pools, and secluded canyons where few anglers ever venture.

A somewhat easier way to fish the canyon of the Florida is found along Forest Road 597. Begin driving this winding dirt road, which is recommended for high-clearance vehicles only. Near the trail to Lost Lake, park just off the road. From this point the Florida Canyon is to the north and west. Contour around the slopes and reach the Florida in about 2 miles of rough walking. Once one is along the river, working upstream is not so difficult as in the stretch below.

The canyon section of the Florida above Transfer Park offers demanding fishing. Not only is the hike into the river arduous, but the high gradient of the stream makes wading difficult. The stream is often narrow and brushy, and casting must be done from tight quarters. A 7-foot rod will help alleviate problems with the brush. Leaders should be kept short, under 7 feet, and use 4X or 5X tippet. Cast dry flies into the heads of plunge pools or around boulders, and seek out pockets of slack water. Nymphs also work well in plunge pools and pockets. Use weighted attractor nymphs like a Pheasant Tail or Hare's Ear, or use beadhead nymphs. For the deepest pools try a weighted streamer fished along the bottom.

In rugged pocket water anglers need dry flies that can take a dunking. Hair-bodied flies work well in the pocket and plunge water. Humpys with yellow, red, or orange thread are an excellent choice for the rough water, as are Irresistibles. Heavy-hackled Wulff patterns in gray, green, or brown also work well. With the abundance of caddis on the stream, the Elk Hair Caddis is often a perfect choice. Use flies in sizes 12 or 14. In early summer, golden stoneflies hatch in the cold, churning water. Small stonefly imitations such as the Stimulator or Yellow Stone on size 12 hooks are effective.

Access to the upper third of the Florida River is easiest from Forest Road 597 and the Endlich Mesa Trail. The trailhead is at the end of Forest Road 597, a long and rough road. The Endlich Mesa Trail leads in 6 miles to City Reservoir and the wide meadows of the Florida below the dam. Only experienced backcountry travelers should attempt this trip because the trail is often difficult to follow. For detailed descriptions of the Endlich Mesa Trail, consult the trail guides for the Weminuche Wilderness or contact the Forest Service office in Durango.

In contrast to the canyon section of the river above Transfer Park, below City Reservoir the Florida flows through a long meadow known as Lowe Park. At 10,600 feet, the setting is spectacular. The stream is twenty feet wide with a rocky bottom as it meanders through the open terrain. Wading and casting are easy in this stretch. Water flowing from the reservoir can be cold, even in mid-summer, and lightweight hip waders are recommended. The fish are spookier in the meadow than below, and 9-foot leaders and 5X or 6X tippet are in order.

Anglers must make delicate casts to fool the trout in the still waters of the meadow. Approach the stream with a low profile and keep casting to a minimum. Cast dry flies along undercut banks, through riffles, and into the heads of pools. Fish more realistic patterns to match the hatches of small mayflies that occur. Along with Parachute Adams in sizes 14 to 18, bring brown, olive, and tan mayfly imitations. Caddis hatches occur in the evening. Try an Elk Hair Caddis, a Royal Trude, or a Goddard Caddis, all in sizes 12 to 16. For fishing below the surface, Muskrat and Hare's Ear nymphs in sizes 12 or 14 are particularly effective.

Above City Reservoir, the Florida is a small stream running through a narrow glacial valley. Glacial moraines impound the stream into several small lakes. In the upper valley the scenery is more attractive than is the fishing for small cut-throats.

Runoff clouds the Florida in May, but the small size of the watershed brings fishable conditions to the river a bit earlier than on other streams in the area. The Florida is often clear by the second week in June. The river is in its prime from June through August and remains good until the end of September.

The difficult fly fishing on the Florida River will not be attractive to every angler, and beginners should take some time to hone their skills on other rivers before going there. Those who are willing to put in the necessary effort to discover its scenic wonders as well as it secret trout holes will be amply rewarded with much more than wild trout.

9

THE ANIMAS AND
LA PLATA WATERSHEDS

ANIMAS RIVER

Managed by: San Juan National Forest, private, City of Durango, Southern Ute Reservation
Access by: Vehicle, foot, and train
Altitude: 5,500 to 12,000 feet
Type of Water: Large river: runs, riffles, pools, pocket water
Best Times: March to April, July to November
Hatches: Caddisflies, pale morning duns, blue-winged olives
Maps: USFS San Juan National Forest; USGS Howardsville, Silverton, Snowdon Peak, Columbine Pass, Electra Lake, Hermosa, Durango East, Loma Linda, Basin Mountain, and Long Mountain 7.5' quadrangles

Evidence of how human perception of the landscape has evolved over the past 250 years is found in contrasting views of the valley of the Animas River. Today the valley and the river itself seem alive, bountiful, and full of beauty. When Juan Rivera passed through this corner of Colorado in 1765, he named the river *El Rio de las Animas Perdidas en Purgatorio*, "The River of the Lost Souls in Hell." To Rivera and his

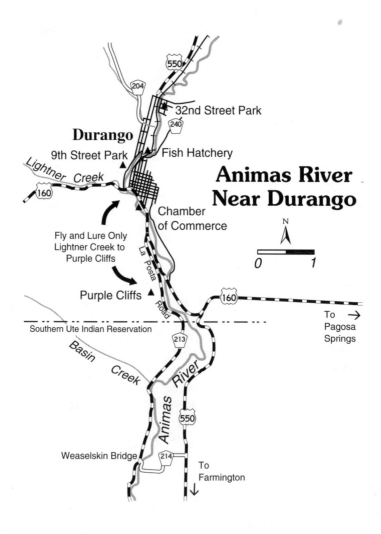

Spanish compatriots, the valley was remote, bleak, and had little to offer them in the way of riches.

Nothing could be further from the truth. The Animas River and its canyons are the centerpiece of southwestern Colorado's burgeoning tourist industry. The Durango and Silverton Narrow Gauge Railroad parallels the Animas the entire way between Silverton and Durango, carrying passengers into the depths of rich forests and along the very brinks of the Animas canyons. Few who come to know the Animas are not touched by the majesty of the river and the surrounding mountains. As for mineral wealth, little did Rivera know that hills enclosing the headwaters of the Animas would produce millions of dollars of silver and gold in the mines around Silverton.

The Animas River is the major stream draining the high alpine terrain of the Needle Mountains. It heads in small meadows on the flanks of Cinnamon Mountain north of Silverton, then plunges through wild canyons as it carves a route between the Needle and West Needle Mountains. By the time it reaches Durango, the Animas has grown to a large river. Out of the mountains the Animas meanders through a shallow depression across broad plains. South of the New Mexico border at Farmington the Animas joins the San Juan River.

The San Juan Mountains surrounding the upper Animas are richly mineralized, and the watershed has a long history of mining for gold, silver, and copper. Low concentrations of heavy metals are found in the water, coming from natural sources and also leaching out of old mine tailings. As a result, the Animas is a dead stream at and above Silverton. Fishing is poor on the upper river, but many of the smaller tributaries around Silverton hold trout.

Beginning with Mineral Creek at the southern end of town, each tributary of the Animas below Silverton has high-quality water and immediately improves conditions in the main stream. The effect of water quality can be dramatically seen in the distribution of fish. Trout in the upper Animas are concentrated where good-quality water enters at the confluences with

The Animas River as seen from above, on the Durango and Silverton Narrow Gauge train. (Photograph courtesy Duranglers, Inc.)

small creeks, and they are sparse in the long stretches in between.

From Elk Park, about 8 miles below Silverton, to Needleton, located halfway to Durango, the river offers fair trout fishing. Flowing within a rugged, deep canyon, the river is difficult to reach. For fly fishing, this area may not be worth the effort it takes to get to the river, but the scenery is spectacular. For a special adventure, consider taking the steam train of the Durango and Silverton Narrow Gauge Railroad from Durango to Needleton. After a two-hour ride, hop off and fish for a couple of hours, then catch the train on its way back from Silverton. Such an excursion requires advance planning and reservations. For a midsummer trip, make arrangements well in advance.

From Cascade Creek downstream the Animas shows steady improvement, but the river doesn't became a fine fishery until it reaches private land in the vicinity of the village of Hermosa. Inflow from Hermosa Creek pushes the water quality of the Animas to the point where the river becomes a stable trout fishery. However, the land along the river from Hermosa Creek to the Durango city limits is all private, and anglers must stay out.

Fortunately, public access to the Animas River within the city of Durango is plentiful from the northern city limit to south of town near the Purple Cliffs. Two parcels of private land are found in this stretch, but they are well marked. Foot and bike trails parallel the river through much of town, providing abundant easy access. Other access points are found at the 9th Street and 32nd Street city parks and at the Colorado Division of Wildlife Fish Hatchery at 151 East 16th Street. In the south part of town along U.S. 160, access is found at the chamber of commerce building and its surrounding public park and extends to the Purple Cliffs. Below Durango the Animas again crosses private land before heading across the Southern Ute Reservation.

The long stretch of river along U.S. 160 from the entrance of Lightner Creek near downtown Durango to the Purple Cliffs is managed as artificial-fly-and-lure-only water with a two-fish limit on fish over 16 inches. Over the past decade special regulations and the closure of several mines on the upper river have made the Animas one of the most improved trout fisheries in the state.

The obvious base of operations for a trip to the Animas is Durango, which offers full-service fly shops and a wide variety of accommodations, restaurants, and other amenities. Private campgrounds are found in and around town, and Forest Service campgrounds are located off U.S. 550 on the way to Silverton.

The Animas is big water. In Durango the river is almost one hundred feet wide, filled with huge rocks and deep holes. The river offers extensive riffles, freestone conditions, and stretches of pocket water. The bottom consists of gravel and cobbles. The rocks are as slick as those in any river in the

West, and anglers must always be very cautious when wading. Wet wading is popular in summer, but waders are called for in the early season and in the fall.

Through town, the Animas flows through a shallow depression. The banks are steep, rocky, and brush-covered, and casting from the bank can be difficult. However, once they are in the stream, anglers will find casting is unobstructed. The size of the river dictates that anglers use a long rod and at least a 5-weight line. Be prepared to make long casts into the wind. Stout tippets and 9-foot leaders work well on the river.

The Animas is home to rainbows, cutthroats, and browns. Annual stocking of catchable-sized rainbows occurs on the river in Durango. In addition, in recent years there have been numerous plantings of brown trout fingerlings and Tasmanian rainbows. The survivors of these efforts are as close to wild fish as you can get. They are strong, smart trout that are doing well in the river.

The big water grows some large fish, and the Animas has a reputation for large trout. Most of the fish in the river are in the 10- to 15-inch range, but the potential for a lunker is real. A past state-record brown trout weighing over twenty pounds was wrestled from the Animas in the 1950s. Fishing for browns is often a difficult proposition involving weighted streamers and hundreds of casts for a few fish. Rainbow fishing is more consistent and offers the dry-fly fishermen a chance to find plenty of good-sized trout.

The Animas experiences a double runoff pattern. As winter ends in March, low elevation snowpack begins to melt and produces high water from early March through early to mid-April. When the high water subsides, the river can offer a couple of weeks of fine spring fishing. Then, when the first warm spell hits in late April or early May, true runoff begins. In a single day the river turns from a friendly stream to a surging mudflow. Fishing is very difficult during high, muddy conditions. Runoff lasts through May and into June and may continue later following winters of high snowpack.

The most important food source for the large trout in the Animas is sculpins. These bottom-dwelling forage fish are found in the mud and rocks throughout the river and are eagerly sought by the trout. The angler can take advantage of this by fishing sculpin patterns along the river bottom. Cast heavily weighted Muddler Minnows or Matuka Muddlers from size 2 to 10 up and across the current, then allow the fly to sink as it moves downstream. Near the bottom of the swing begin a slow retrieve, bouncing the fly along the rocks. Hold on for what could be some real excitement if a monster brown grabs your sculpin!

Caddisflies are the most important aquatic insect in the Animas. Hatches begin around June 1, when they are usually masked by the later stages of runoff. The trout will actively feed if the water is high and clear, and they will often take caddis even when the water is muddy. Caddis hatches continue all summer long but tail off as the season progresses. Evening dry-fly fishing can be excellent in July and August with Elk Hair, Goddard Caddis, or Trude patterns. In early summer use a size 12 or 14 pattern. By August the caddisflies are smaller, calling for the same patterns but in sizes 18 or 20. Look for naturals on the water or vegetation, and use the appropriately sized fly. When fishing in the evening, imitate egg-laying female caddisflies by casting a fly, then skittering it with quick jumps across the surface. This action often brings a slashing rise from a trout. Nymphing with caddis larva or pupa patterns is also good throughout the summer. Use cased caddis or olive, gray, or muskrat patterns in sizes 12 to 16.

Another effective way to catch trout where caddisflies are present is fishing in traditional wet-fly style. Tie on a soft-hackle pattern or a Western Coachman, with or without a small amount of weight on the leader. Cast upstream a few feet, let the fly sink, then, without mending the line, let the fly swing across and up the current at the end of the drift. Many adult caddisflies lay eggs while swimming under the water, and this technique imitates the actions of these insects.

A midsummer hatch of pale morning duns stimulates trout feeding in the Animas. The hatch occurs late-morning from July until early August. Match the hatch with size 16 or 18 pale-bodied flies, such as a Light Cahill or any of the specifically designed Pale Morning Dun patterns. Size 16 to 18 nymphs—either a Pheasant Tail or dark Hare's Ear—are effective before and during the hatch. Note, however, that by midafternoon in midsummer, water temperatures are often high and the fish seek out deeper water until evening again cools the water down.

When no hatch is on, first try fishing weighted nymphs or dropping sculpin patterns along the bottom. Prince Nymphs are also a proven general attractor pattern for the Animas. If these ideas fail to work, hopper patterns are an excellent alternative. Particularly effective is a Dry Muddler in sizes 8 to 12 skittered over the surface.

Fly fishing can remain excellent on the Animas through the snows of early November. The crisp, clear days of autumn, tinted with yellow aspens on the mountain slopes, offer ideal angling weather. Many anglers throughout the San Juans consider September and October the best months to be on the Animas, as well as other rivers in the area. Although there is less surface action in the fall, dry flies cast to rising trout will often bring fine results. Watch for late fall hatches of blue-winged olives and midge activity, which can occur around midday in October and November. When all else fails, try a Little Brown Trout, Matuka, or your favorite streamer pattern fished along the bottom.

Below the Purple Cliffs the Animas runs through private land and the Southern Ute Indian Reservation. Some tribal land along La Posta Road is open to angling for those with a Southern Ute Reservation permit. For details on the location of the water, consult the latest edition of the Southern Ute Indian Reservation Fishing Proclamation.

On Southern Ute land the Animas remains a cold-water fishery and still holds plenty of trout. Most attractive are the large brown trout found in this stretch, but rainbows are also found here. In the last few years Snake River cutthroat trout have been stocked by the Southern Utes. It is often difficult to work your way through the small cutthroats to get at the bigger browns, but it is always worth the effort.

A few miles below Durango, the river character changes. The channel has fewer big boulders and more flat water. The river is more prone to be off-color below than above, and since a 1994 fire in the drainage of a small tributary on the west side of the river, it takes little rain to muddy the flow.

In this stretch are good populations of caddisflies and sculpins. Fishing is often best in late summer and early fall with Woolly Buggers in black, brown, and olive, Muddler Minnows, and Matuka Muddlers. When streamer fishing, start at the top of a run and cast across the current. Add an upstream mend to the line and the fly will sink quickly. Swing and point your rod tip downstream and begin to strip in the fly with one- to two-foot pulls on the line. Continue stripping the fly back across the current, always in a down-and-across motion. Be certain to work around any boulders in the middle of the river by letting the fly sink a little by the boulder, then continue to strip the pattern in. Watch carefully for strikes when your pattern is sinking and when you again begin the stripping motion. This technique can work wonders on the large brown trout found in the river.

Since 1995 the stretch of the Animas from Basin Creek to Weaselskin Bridge has been managed for trophy fish. It is fly-and-lure-only water with a two-fish limit, and the fish must be over 16 inches. Smaller fish must be released.

For many, the attraction of the Animas is the ease of access in and around Durango. There is a certain, almost rustic charm to fishing within sight of the houses on the bluffs above the river or to casting while the steam train rumbles by. But don't be deceived into thinking fishing the Animas is easy. The big water is rough, and it takes hard work to pull a trout from it. The Animas is one river that will make you pay your dues.

CASCADE AND LIME CREEKS

Managed by: San Juan National Forest
Access by: Vehicle and foot
Altitude: 6,200 to 11,800 feet
Type of Water: Small streams, meadow water, rugged canyon pocket water
Best Times: July to September
Hatches: Caddisflies, mayflies, yellow stoneflies
Maps: USFS San Juan National Forest; USGS Snowden Peak, Engineer Mountain, and Electra Lake 7.5' quadrangles

Cascade and Lime Creeks, two of the northernmost major tributaries of the Animas River, offer the angler picturesque small-stream fly fishing. Water quality in both creeks is good, and both hold fine populations of brown, brook, cutbow, and rainbow trout. For those in the Durango area looking for some relaxing fishing away from the road, these two creeks are a good bet. For anglers willing to explore a bit, these streams can offer some special secret places.

Lime Creek heads south of Silverton at the foot of Twin Sisters and Bear Mountains. Below U.S. 550 the stream is paralleled by Forest Road 591 first heading south, then bending sharply to the west to rejoin U.S. 550. Access to Lime Creek along Forest Road 591 is easy in places and very difficult in others. Trouble-free access is restricted to the south-heading stretch; when the creek turns west it plunges into a narrow rugged canyon where walking is difficult and dangerous all the way down to the confluence with Cascade Creek at Purgatory Flats.

The upper stretch of Cascade Creek flows for 10 miles through the mountains before crossing U.S. 550. Just above the highway a diversion dam drains away much of the flow of the creek, but enough water remains to support a few trout below the highway. About 3 miles below the diversion Lime Creek joins Cascade at Purgatory Flats.

Access to both creeks is via U.S. 550 about 25 miles north of Durango. Upper Cascade Creek is reached from a four-wheel-drive road about 2 miles north of Purgatory Ski Area. Turn left onto the road and drive as far as you can on this rough road, or begin walking. The road, which soon turns into a trail, follows the creek several miles upstream.

To reach Lime Creek, go 2 miles north of the Purgatory Ski Area and turn right onto Forest Road 591. This road is rough with several steep sections, and although high clearance is recommended, four-wheel-drive is not required to make the complete trip. Drive the road, search for easy access, and avoid the sheer drops into the canyon.

Hike-in access to fine fishing on Cascade and Lime Creeks is via the Purgatory Trail #511 to Purgatory Flats. The trailhead is on U.S. 550 just across from the Purgatory Ski Area. The trail drops 800 feet in the first 1.5 miles: Allow forty minutes to reach Cascade Creek and at least an hour to make the climb back to the trailhead. At the flats, anglers have three choices: You can fish downstream into the rugged box canyon of Cascade Creek as it drops 400 feet to the Animas River; you can choose to fish some low-gradient water in Purgatory Flats; or you can walk upstream about a mile to the confluence of Cascade and Lime Creeks, then fish either small stream.

In the vicinity of Purgatory Flats both Lime and Cascade Creeks are between fifteen and twenty feet wide. This is tumbling water over a rocky, clean streambed. Although it sounds as if the flats should hold meadow water, the area is forested. The stream banks are brushy, and casting can be done from within the streams themselves. Anglers need to wade to fish effectively. The streams are easily wadable except in the rugged country of the lower box canyon on Cascade Creek and upstream on Lime Creek. Wet wading is fine in midsummer, but carry hip waders in the early season and the fall.

Lime Creek holds plenty of fish, mostly in the 6- to 10-inch range. Small brook and rainbow trout are found in the upper portion of Cascade Creek. Scattered larger fish are found in the excellent pocket water below the confluence of Lime and Cascade.

These small streams are swollen with runoff in April and May, with the water usually dropping by mid-June. They can produce well throughout the summer and into early October. Below the confluence, fall fishing can be productive to November, depending on the weather.

Both streams have a variety of caddis, stoneflies, and mayflies. Many times the water will light up with multiple hatches during midsummer evenings. Thin mayfly hatches occur on Cascade Creek. Yellow and green stoneflies are important in early summer on Lime Creek, particularly in the canyon sections. Try casting Stimulators or Lime Trude patterns in sizes 10 to 16. Caddis larva patterns are a good choice throughout the summer. Dry flies can be effective almost any time. For dry-fly fishing, try Elk Hair Caddis, House and Lot Variant, Humpy, and Irresistible in sizes 12 to 16. Fish dry flies in the choppy water and along undercut banks in the short meadow stretches.

When fishing below the surface, use attractor nymph patterns with a small amount of lead on the leader. Another surprisingly effective small-stream technique to try here is to fish with a dropper. Select a high-floating dry fly from size 10 to 14 and tie a smaller weighted nymph, perhaps a size 16 Prince Nymph or a Pheasant Tail to the bend of the dry-fly hook, using a foot to 18 inches of tippet between the two flies. In the course of the day both flies will take their share of fish.

HERMOSA CREEK

Managed by: San Juan National Forest
Access by: Vehicle, foot, and mountain bike
Altitude: 6,600 to 11,200 feet
Type of Water: Small stream, meadow water, pocket water
Best Times: July to September
Hatches: Caddisflies, stoneflies, mayflies
Maps: USFS San Juan National Forest; USGS Hermosa
    Peak, Engineer Mountain, Elk Creek, Monument Hill, and
    Hermosa 7.5' quadrangles

Hermosa Creek is a major tributary of the Animas River
that drains a huge area of forested mountains west of the Animas Valley. The San Juan Mountains' best combination
mountain bike and fishing excursion is a trip along Hermosa
Creek. About 20 miles of stream are available along the long
Hermosa Creek Trail, which is open to hikers, horseback riders, mountain bikes, and motorcycles. With so much stream
to cover, a mountain bike is the perfect mode of transporta-
tion to reach the middle section of the creek.

Lower Hermosa Creek is accessible on Forest Road 576
about 10 miles north of Durango. Public land begins about 4
miles up this road, but the road stays away from the stream,
and access to the creek requires a bit of a hike. To reach Hermosa Creek from the north, take U.S. 550 about 30 miles
north of Durango to just beyond the Purgatory Ski Area. Turn
left onto Forest Road 578. Climb steeply over a divide to
reach the East Fork of Hermosa Creek. The trailhead for the
Hermosa Creek Trail is about 12 miles from U.S. 550.

The East Fork of Hermosa Creek offers the rare opportunity to fish for native Colorado River cutthroats. In 1992,
brook trout were removed from the stream and cutthroats
were brought in from a nearby natural population. This

stretch provides the easiest access to Colorado River cutthroat fishing in southern Colorado. From Sig Creek Campground to the headwaters the East Fork is managed as fly-and-lure-only catch-and-release water. The fish are generally small, ranging from 5 to 10 inches. Please be especially careful with these rare and delicate fish.

The East Fork is a tiny stream averaging two or three feet in width and about a foot in depth. It is slow, meandering meadow water with a glasslike surface. The banks are not grassy but are brush-lined. The cutthroats are extremely spooky. These conditions add up to highly technical fly fishing in which presentation is critical. The difficult angling found in this stretch is not for everyone, and beginners are sure to find it frustrating.

On the East Fork, pull out the 6X or 7X tippet. Always make a cautious approach to the stream (and crawling on hands and knees would not be an extreme measure). Keep casting to a minimum. The best technique is to fish downstream, drifting a fly under vegetation, to undercut banks, and even around corners. A variety of patterns will work, but small ant and beetle patterns, sizes 14 to 18, are particularly effective. Small mayfly patterns often do the trick when a hatch is present. Midges can be productive in the evening.

Upstream from the confluence of the East Fork and the main Hermosa Creek, Forest Road 578 continues to parallel the stream. Four-wheel-drive is required to make a stream crossing to follow the stream to its headwaters near the Graysill Mine. Good fly fishing can be found in this stretch in areas that are located away from the road. The main fork is a bit larger than the East Fork and is about five feet in width. Brook and rainbow trout are the most prevalent trout species, and most fish are in the 7- to 10-inch range.

To find more fishing holes, head downstream from the confluence with the East Fork along the Hermosa Creek Trail. You will find plenty of access points along the trail, but the trail is often on the slopes above and away from the stream, particularly in the canyon section in the middle miles of this long stretch.

The stream gains size as it descends toward the Animas. Anglers will find meadow water, long riffles, and in the central canyon section plenty of pocket water. More deep holes are found in this area than in any other stretch of the stream. A variety of conditions are found, from open banks to tight brushy stretches. The stream is big enough to get into and make roll casts to likely trout lies.

Mostly rainbow and brook trout are found in the central stretch. Many cutbow hybrids are also found in the stream, along with an occasional brown. Most fish are in the 8- to 12-inch range, with a few up to 16 inches hiding in protected locations.

Typical small-stream flies and techniques are used on the central section of Hermosa. With the trout notably unfussy, high-floating impressionistic patterns work well. Humpys, Royal Wulffs, and Irresistibles in sizes 12 to 16 are best in the foamy pocket-water stretches. For quieter water, try an Adams, a Grizzly Wulff, or any small mayfly imitation in sizes 14 to 18. Float dry flies along the banks and under over-hanging vegetation. A good place to look for trout is at the junctions with the many side streams that join the Hermosa along the way.

About 5 miles above the junction with the Animas, Hermosa Creek flows through another short canyon. Here the access trail is far above the stream. Steep canyon walls make access difficult in this stretch. Most anglers skip this stretch to fish the stream above.

Snow keeps Hermosa Creek inaccessible until the beginning of runoff in May. High flows continue until mid-June. July, August, and September are the premier months on the river, but conditions generally remain good until October.

A mountain bike excursion into Hermosa Creek requires some careful planning. From the confluence with the East Fork to U.S. 550 is 24 miles of uphill and downhill riding. A strong rider could do the trip in four hours, not counting time for angling. Only experienced riders who can handle narrow, rocky single track should attempt the complete trip. Be prepared for some steep climbing over the last 8 miles of the trail. For the less energetic, an alternative is to ride in from the upper trailhead 5 or 6 miles, fish for a while, then return by the same route. The return trip will be an uphill grind, so save plenty of energy.

Animas Watershed Lakes

Unlike the neighboring drainages in the high country of the Weminuche Wilderness, the Animas watershed is not loaded with lakes. However, the Animas lakes offer easier access, and often the fishing and the scenery are just as grand as in more remote areas. There is a trade-off, of course. You should expect to see a few more fellow anglers in lakes close to the highway.

Three lakes sit along U.S. 550 a few miles south of Silverton, each at about 10,500 feet. The private Molas Lake is adjacent to the highway about 5 miles south of Silverton and 40 miles north of Durango. Molas is the largest of the three lakes and offers good fishing for a fee. A mile south of Molas Lake is the turnoff to Little Molas Lake on the west side of the

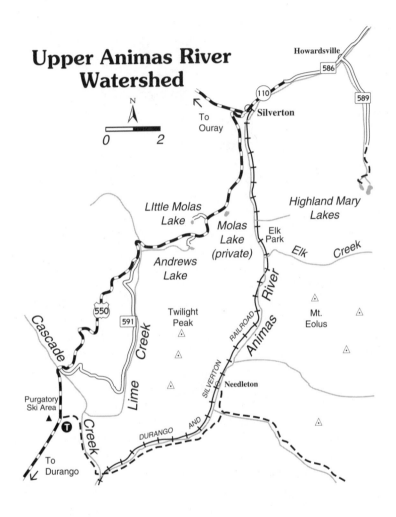

Upper Animas River Watershed

N

0   2

Howardsville

586

589

110

To
Ouray

Silverton

LIttle Molas
Lake

Highland Mary
Lakes

Molas
Lake
(private)

Elk
Park

Elk Creek

Andrews
Lake

550

591

Twilight
Peak

River

Mt.
Eolus

Cascade

Lime Creek

RAILROAD

Animas

Creek

SILVERTON

Needleton

Purgatory
Ski Area

DURANGO

AND

To
Durango

highway. A 1-mile dirt road leads to the lake. The turnoff to
Andrews Lake is a mile south of Molas Pass. The lake is less
than a mile from the highway on an all-weather road. The
road to Little Molas is easy for all vehicles but is muddy in
early summer, when those without four-wheel-drive might
consider walking the short distance into the lake.

No special regulations are in effect for any of these lakes. They offer stocked rainbow and brook trout with a few good fish in the 12-inch range. The lakes are ideal for float tubes and are surprisingly scenic spots for fly fishing, particularly in the early morning when the sun eases up over the Needle Mountains to the east.

The Molas area lakes have thin hatches of caddisflies, and adult caddis or larva patterns in sizes 10 to 16 are often very effective. Cast to rising fish, or allow larva or pupa patterns to sink, then pull them slowly toward the surface. Damselflies can be important in the early summer. The most consistent flies for the lakes are streamers. Matukas, bucktails, and other streamers should be fished at various depths to find where the trout are feeding.

Closer to Durango, Haviland Lake is about 20 miles north of town off U.S. 550. Turn right (east) toward Chris Park and Haviland Lake Campgrounds. The entire lake is on public land. The lake is heavily stocked with rainbow trout each year and offers easy access to good stillwater fishing. Trout feed on damselflies and midges. Fishing patterns to imitate these food sources from the bank or a float tube can provide a good day of fun fishing. Try olive damselfly nymphs, Tellico nymphs, and Western Coachmen. The season begins on Haviland Lake in May and continues through September.

The private Electra Lake is just north of Haviland Lake. Electra holds one of the finest populations of brook trout in Colorado along with some cutthroats and rainbows. A small fee is charged per day to fish the lake. Fishing is best from boats, but there is some bank fishing for those who want to try for a fat brookie. The lake is rather large and is not suitable for float tubes. *Callibaetis* hatches occur throughout the summer. Shrimp and midges are other important food sources for the trout, as are young fish. The best bet for the fly fisherman is size 6 to 10 bucktail streamers imitating trout fry. Fish streamers deep or along the surface. Electra Lake opens up in May, and fishing continues to be good through September.

The most interesting lakes in the Animas watershed are the Highland Mary Lakes above Silverton. The lakes are timberline lakes within the Weminuche Wilderness with relatively easy access. From Silverton, take Colorado 110 north until it turns to gravel and joins Forest Road 586. Drive another 2 miles to Howardsville and turn right on Forest Road 589. The first 2 miles of this road are negotiable with any vehicle, but the last 3 miles require a four-wheel-drive. From the trailhead it is 2 miles and a 1,200-foot climb to the first of the lakes.

Three lakes are located in the basin at 12,000 feet, and the Verde Lakes are found about a mile beyond. Angling from the bank or a float tube is possible in each of the lakes. Much of the summer, midges are the most important insects. In midsummer, come prepared to match the *Callibaetis* hatch. A long rod will help in getting flies out to the fish cruising around offshore.

LA PLATA RIVER

Managed by: San Juan National Forest
Access by: Vehicle
Altitude: 8,500 to 10,500 feet
Type of Water: Small freestone stream with pocket water
Best Times: July to September
Hatches: Mayflies and caddis
Maps: San Juan National Forest; USGS Hesperus and La Plata 7.5' quadrangles

When Juan Rivera led his party of Spaniards from Santa Fe into southern Colorado, he sought to confirm tales of gold and silver located in the unknown mountains north of the San Juan River. West of the Animas River, he camped along a stream draining from a cluster of snowcapped peaks. He named both the mountains and the stream *La Plata* in hopes

of finding silver ore within the drainage. Rivera never found any sign of the precious metal he desired.

The La Plata River is probably the smallest stream in southern Colorado that is called a river. Only twenty feet wide at its greatest breadth, the La Plata drains the abrupt peaks of the La Plata Mountains, the southwesternmost of the ranges of the San Juans. It is a short river, less than 40 miles long. The watershed too is small, keeping the La Plata not much more than a creek for most of its public stretch.

U.S. 160 crosses the La Plata about 10 miles west of Durango at the village of Hesperus. From Hesperus, the paved County Road 124 parallels the La Plata through Mayday, where the road becomes all-weather gravel. This good road continues upstream another 8 miles before turning rougher and changing its designation to Forest Road 498. Above, a four-wheel-drive road parallels the upper river to Kennebec Pass. Several Forest Service campgrounds are located along the road.

South of Mayday the La Plata flows entirely on private land. The public section of the La Plata above Mayday flows through a rocky forested canyon where fishing can be difficult.

Easy access along the road is limited and anglers will find themselves clambering over rocks and through the forest to reach likely places to fish. The river often tumbles through a narrow gorge, where getting to and traveling along the stream requires caution. The high gradient of the river produces plunge pools and pocket water where many boulders are found in the stream. The river frequently flows over bedrock. Except in the pools the river is shallow enough to wade almost everywhere.

Anglers will want to carry short rods to work the La Plata. Rocks and streamside vegetation conspire to make tight conditions, and casting is often difficult. Anglers will find that flip, roll, and sidearm casts are most useful in avoiding snags on the riparian vegetation. Hip boots will always be sufficient for fishing the La Plata.

The cascading currents of the La Plata hold plenty of small trout. Brown and rainbow trout are found in the lower reaches of public water just above Mayday. Brook trout become more common as one moves upstream. In the tiny headwaters a 10-inch fish is a prize, but farther downstream skilled anglers will find an occasional brown trout up to 14 inches. No special regulations are in effect on the La Plata.

The La Plata watershed gathers a huge quantity of winter snows, creating a dramatic runoff. Fishing is difficult on the river from mid-May through late June. After runoff the river runs clear throughout summer and fall. The river fishes well from July to early September.

Stoneflies are common in the river, but the large hatches of the insects are generally masked by high runoff. A few species of mayfly are found in the La Plata, and hatches usually occur in midsummer around midday. Cloudy weather often enhances the hatches. The trout generally do not key into one species when feeding, but fishing an appropriately sized Adams or Brown Wulff during a hatch might increase the chances of success. Caddis are also found in the river, and caddis patterns are effective in summer. In the swift currents of much of the La Plata attractor drys are all that are required.

When fishing the small pocket water on the La Plata, select a high-floating, high-visibility fly such as a Humpy or one of the Wulffs. Ignore the choppy, foaming water. Put the fly on the water wherever the currents are slack: behind and in front of boulders, along edges, and in current seams. The trick is to keep most of the fly line off the water so that the swift currents won't drag the fly out of the slower water. To do this, use your arm to hold the tip of the rod high off the water. Use as little line as possible, fishing with mostly leader and tippet. Long graceful casts are useless; get up close to your target and flip the fly into the slack water. Even a couple of seconds of float may be enough. In fast currents trout don't have much time to make up their minds about a food item.

10

THE DOLORES WATERSHED

DOLORES RIVER BELOW MCPHEE RESERVOIR

Managed by: San Juan National Forest, Colorado Department of Wildlife, Bureau of Land Management
Access by: Vehicle
Altitude: 6,700 to 7,100 feet
Type of Water: Tailwater fishery
Best Times: June to October
Hatches: Blue-winged olive, pale morning duns, caddisflies
Maps: USFS San Juan National Forest; USGS Doe Canyon, Yellow Jacket, and Trimble Point 7.5' quadrangles

When McPhee Dam was completed in 1983 it initiated a chain of events that have led to new angling opportunities, disappointments, misconceptions, and controversies that continue more than a decade later. Impounding the Dolores River, the dam is the keystone of a wide-ranging irrigation project designed to deliver unlimited quantities of water to the bean fields of the high rolling hills north of Cortez. A by-product was the creation of a tailwater fishery on the Dolores that

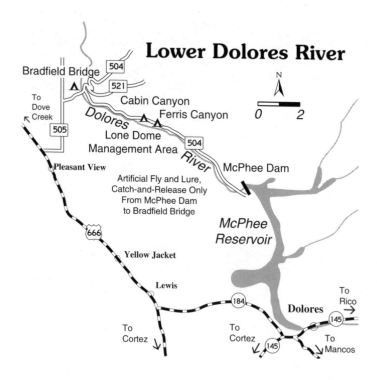

once was, and it is hoped will be again, a premier tailwater fishery in Colorado.

As water began flowing from McPhee Reservoir into the Dolores Canyon below the dam, the trout fishery in the river was reborn. Even though the Dolores is considered by many to be a desert river, it flows freely with snowmelt from the western half of the San Juans and even at the site of the dam is at an elevation of 7,100 feet. Written records show trout were present in this section of the Dolores as recently as the early part of this century. Beginning in the 1930s, diversion projects took the water from the Dolores and sent it south to the agricultural fields around Cortez. So much water was

Cool water temperatures and moderate flows can make fall a prime time to fish the long tailwater on the Dolores River below McPhee Dam. (Photograph by Craig Martin.)

taken from the river that it frequently ran dry in summer below the town of Dolores, and the trout fishery was destroyed.

Before cold water again flowed through the Dolores canyon—this time coming from deep beneath the surface of McPhee Reservoir—Colorado Division of Wildlife saw the potential for a fine trout fishery. When cold water from the reservoir was first released into the river channel in 1983, CDOW stocked ten thousand fingerlings each of brown, rainbow, and Snake River cutthroat trout, and the rebirth of the Dolores was on its way. Since the beginning, CDOW has imposed special regulations on the river: artificial flies and lures only, and catch-and-release for the first 12 miles of river below the dam.

The fishery developed with amazing speed, but under conditions that would soon prove to be misleading. In 1984, summer flows below the dam never dropped below 200 to 250 cfs, providing plenty of habitat for the new trout populations. Three major factors kept water levels higher than could normally be expected under the management plan for the reservoir. First, the closing of the dam was followed by several wet years and above-normal precipitation that quickly filled the reservoir. Second, the method of operation of the dam also helped keep water levels high. Unlike most reservoirs, where water is sent through the dam to be taken from the river at points downstream, McPhee is operated like Navajo Reservoir—water for irrigation is pulled directly from the impoundment. Finally, much of the irrigation water delivery system was incomplete. Reservoir levels and river flows remained higher than could be expected under more developed irrigation.

With consistent high flows, from 1984 to 1986 the Dolores acquired its reputation as a world-class tailwater fishery. During these years the river saw minimum flows of 78 cfs only for short periods of time. Word spread quickly, and anglers from all over the region flocked to the river to catch its fast-growing wild trout. Anglers and fisheries managers were as happy as a brown trout during a stonefly hatch.

But the Dolores and McPhee Reservoir had not yet experienced a normal year. The river had not been forced to yield water to irrigators according to the conditions under which the dam had been built. Under the comprehensive management plan, minimum flows for the year were determined on March 1. The flow volume was established by estimating the reservoir level that would occur on the last day of June. Irrigation demands and the river would share the water proportionally, with the larger percentage going to agriculture. Depending on the estimate, the minimum flow was set at either 78 cfs, 50 cfs, or 20 cfs.

When a long drought hit in 1987, flow into the reservoir dropped dramatically. At the same time, the irrigation water delivery system was partially completed and water from the reservoir headed to surrounding agricultural fields. Because of the drought conditions, flows in the river remained at 78 cfs for longer periods of time than in the previous 4 years.

The effect of 78 cfs on the trout population was immediate. From 1987 through 1989 the fishery in the Dolores shrank to the carrying capacity of 78 cfs. The fine reputation that the river had acquired in 1986 was no longer representative of the new conditions and many anglers went away disappointed. By 1989 the river had again stabilized as a quality fishery, but it was not the same as in 1986. The river held good numbers of trout, and the fish grew to nice size. Anglers adjusted their expectations to the new conditions and eventually accepted the new, less-productive Dolores.

In 1990 the inevitable happened. On March 1 it was determined minimum flow for the year would be 20 cfs. The gates were closed down, and for over one hundred days flow from the dam remained at 20 cfs, far too little water to maintain trout. To accentuate the problem, spring and summer that year were the warmest of the recent past. From 40 to 60 percent of the trout in the river perished before public pressure brought managers and water users to reevaluate the 20 cfs determination. Flows were increased to 50 cfs. If the river had been managed strictly by the book and flows had remained at 20 cfs until March of the following year, an estimated 90 percent of the Dolores trout would have been lost.

The lesson learned from 1990 was that a flow of 20 cfs will not maintain a quality trout fishery below McPhee Dam. Acting quickly, a local group of concerned parties pushed for the organization of the Dolores Optimization Committee. Representatives of the Bureau of Reclamation, the Dolores Water Conservancy District, the Bureau of Land Management, the Forest Service, the Colorado Division of Wildlife, Colorado Trout Unlimited, and the water user boards sat on the committee. Seeking a change in the management strategy more conducive to trout, the committee arrived at the "pool" concept as an interim plan. In pool management, minimum flow determinations were eliminated and variable flows were introduced. In short, variable flow pushes the same amount of water through the system but changes the volume and timing of high and low flows. The purpose of variable flow was to maintain water for the irrigators and to insure there was always adequate water flowing through the dam for the trout downstream.

Since pool management was introduced, the river has done better with less water. Careful management of flow timing makes a huge difference. Generally, more water goes into the river in summer than in winter. Winter flows can be expected to range between 30 and 40 cfs, while summer flows tend to be in the 70 to 90 cfs range. Spring flows can sit at a low 50 cfs to a high of up to 5,000. Flows are dependent on the depth of winter snowpack and water conditions in the reservoir.

Variable water flows have brought the Dolores fishery back to near 1989 levels. As of 1996, trout remain fewer and smaller than those in 1989, but there is some visible improvement each year. The river has seen an increase in brown trout, while cutthroats seem to have taken the low-water years the hardest. Currently the Dolores holds a good population of fish in the 12- to 16-inch range, with some fish over 20 inches.

The pool-management concept seems to work on the Dolores. In any case, variable flows are better than having a major disruption of the fishery every seven years on the average—the mean frequency of the occurrence of drought conditions. At present the concept is still being negotiated. As one can tell from this complex story of river management, conditions on the river may remain constant for many years or they may quickly change.

Despite the history of uses and abuses, the Dolores remains a fine stream. The first 12 miles below McPhee Dam—all the way to Bradfield Bridge—are managed as catch-and-release water, and all hooked trout must immediately be returned to the river. Angling is limited to artificial flies and lures only. Many of the browns, rainbows, and rainbow hybrids are wild fish, but occasional stocking of fingerlings currently helps maintain the trout population.

Driving into the Dolores on the straight, dusty gravel roads from the highway gives no clue that a trout stream can be found within 50 miles. On the brake-scorching descent of the canyon wall from the rolling hills of the plateau, the shimmer of the green leaves of the cottonwoods along the river provides the first indication that water is nearby. Deep within the canyon the rest of the world seems to disappear from sight and mind. The Dolores threads its way over the wide floor of the gorge. Behind the shining water are white cliffs of sandstone composed of the telltale swirling lines of ancient sand dunes from the time of the dinosaurs. Above the bare rock, sloping walls covered with green fade back from the river. In the fall the walls turn red as the oaks feel the coming of winter and, along with the yellow willows and cottonwoods streamside, paint a backdrop for angling as pretty as any in Colorado.

To reach the Dolores below McPhee Dam from Durango, take U.S. 160 west 28 miles to Mancos and turn right onto Highway 184. In 18 miles, turn left at the intersection with Highway 145, then, in less than a mile, turn right back onto Colorado 184. In another 8 miles turn right onto U.S. 666. Nine miles up U.S. 666, near the village of Pleasant View, bear right onto Forest Road 505, on which are signs for the Dolores River. In a mile this road jogs left; stay on the road another 5 miles to Bradfield Bridge. Across the bridge turn right onto Forest Road 504, which parallels the river to the dam.

The land adjacent to the Dolores between McPhee Dam and Bradfield Bridge is managed cooperatively by the State of Colorado and the Forest Service as part of the Lone Dome Management Area. Several small campgrounds are found in this area. Basic services are available in the town of Dove Creek on U.S. 666. More extensive facilities are found 40 miles from the river in Cortez.

Easy access to the Dolores helps maintain its popularity, and with 12 miles of water it is easy for anglers to find their own piece of river. Below the dam, the river flows through a wide sandstone canyon bordered by rock cliffs. The walls of the canyon are covered with juniper and piñon woodlands, but the canyon itself supports a variety of vegetation ranging from cottonwood to sagebrush to Douglas fir. It is a user-friendly stream with easy wading, low gradients, and plenty of room to work into position and make a cast. There is not much pocket water on the river, but it has many shallow riffles and slow turns. During low summer flows holding water is scattered and the angler will have to cover a long section of river in the course of the day.

The temperamental nature of the river creates conditions where it is not always easy to catch fish. Trout get long looks at a fly before deciding whether or not to take it. Although matching the hatch is usually the most productive method for catching trout, there are times when the fish will take anything. Experienced anglers tend to love the challenge of the Dolores; novice anglers often have a tough time.

Light- to midweight rods are best suited for this tailwater. Three- to 5-weight outfits are ideal, and 8½- to 9-foot rods work well. Because the river is not fast nor deep, there is no need to cast heavily weighted leaders, so powerful stiff rods are not required. The cold water temperatures usually associated with tailwaters are felt only for the first mile or so downstream from the dam. Light hip waders or wet wading will carry you through late spring to summer. For cooler weather, light hip boots are usually sufficient.

Most fishermen on the Dolores are found near the dam, but you don't have to join the throng to have a fine day on the river. If you feel crowded at the upper end, consider dropping down a few miles. With 12 miles of river, you can find a place to be alone on the water. Going in midweek will increase your chances of having a long stretch of river to yourself. Because it is a small and popular river, a few groups can make a crowd. Most anglers on the river are respectful of others. Be courteous by giving other anglers plenty of room, and do not follow other fishermen too closely.

The first few weeks following runoff is a prime time to be on the Dolores. Fishing is noticeably slower in the heat of summer, but it picks up again in the fall. In general, cloudy

When fishing the Dolores River, search for subtle structure in the river—current seams, submerged rocks, hidden undercuts, and pillows of slack water in front of boulders are areas trout favor. (Photograph by Craig Martin.)

days are best. Begin your day by fishing nymphs in the morning, waiting for the hatches that usually occur in late morning and early afternoon. By late afternoon fishing is usually tough, but watch for a flurry of activity just before dark. As temperatures drop in the fall, fishing is best at midday.

Dry flies are the most popular way to fish the Dolores. It is best to try to match the hatch and fish to rising trout. Most hatches are more intense near the dam and become sporadic lower down. This can work against you because there can be so many insects on the water near the dam that fishing is difficult.

Pale morning dun hatches occur in midsummer in the late morning. The light-colored mayflies are well imitated with a Comparadun or a simple yellow-tan parachute fly in sizes 16 to 18. Caddisflies are also important on the Dolores, but hatches of these insects are not predictable or consistent. Adult caddis patterns are effective when the naturals are on the water. Stoneflies are not common in the river, but anglers will find some golden stoneflies and yellow sallies on the water in early summer.

The blue-winged olive is the most consistent hatch on the river. Hatches are most numerous in spring and fall, but summer hatches are not uncommon, particularly on overcast days. The insects range from size 18 to 24. Cast a Blue-Winged Olive dry fly to rising fish or use it as a searching pattern. Small olive or dark nymphs are equally effective during and after the hatch.

In season, terrestrials are particularly effective on the Dolores. Ants and beetles are frequently found on the water, making foam beetles and ant patterns a good choice at any time of the year. Carry patterns ranging from size 10 to 16. Larger patterns are more effective early in the year. Grasshopper season runs from June to midfall. Large hopper patterns in sizes 6 to 10 are particularly good fished along the banks. Dave's Hoppers, Joe's Hoppers, and parachute hopper patterns have repeatedly proven their worth by bringing nice trout to the surface.

Attractor patterns also have their time and place on the Dolores. When fishing below the surface, try a Prince Nymph or a Hare's Ear in sizes 10 to 14. Caddis larvae are consistent producers in green, tan, and gray. On the surface, try a House and Lot or Parachute Adams in sizes 12 to 18. It is considered bad form to show up to fish the Dolores without a half-dozen Royal Wulffs in size 16.

By late September the insects on the river are small. A size 24 blue-winged olive is the main hatch through November, and thin to heavy midday hatches make the trout active feeders. In the absence of a hatch, attractors are a good choice after midday. Select a smaller pattern than you would in summer, using patterns from size 14 to 18. On sunny warm days, look for grasshoppers on the streamside vegetation, and if you find a few, pop a big hopper pattern into the deep runs. Below the surface, large populations of dace and sculpins make streamers an effective method of fishing the Dolores. In fact, these patterns are a good choice at any time.

In winter the river generally freezes over. Open water near the dam cannot be reached by vehicle because the road is closed to protect wintering elk. From December 1 to April 1 each year a locked gate blocks access about 3.5 miles below the dam. Anglers can reach the open water on foot, cross-country skis, or on a mountain bike.

Runoff is generally too high and fast for angling, and the water is usually off-color. During runoff the fish are scattered and hard to find, adding to the difficulties for the fly fisherman. High water can last from April to early-to-late June depending on winter snowfall and spring rains.

For a different angling adventure you can try the Dolores below Bradfield Bridge. The catch-and-release designation stops at the bridge, but there are still some brown trout and rainbows downstream. The first section below the bridge gets pounded hard, but the canyon extends for many miles. It is strictly walk-in water with no other access for 18 miles. Attempt a trip into this wild country only if you are fully prepared.

Another way to experience this lower water is with an experienced guide service. As runoff declines, overnight float fishing trips are an option. Although it's hard to believe from the parts of the river visible from the road, the lower Dolores is tree-lined with five-hundred-plus-year-old Douglas firs and ponderosa pines. Combined with the red rock canyon walls up to 800 feet high, Anasazi ruins, and some awesome fish, this float trip is well worth the time. Contact Duranglers at (970) 385-4081, or Telluride Outside at (970) 728-3895 for more information.

Even with a checkered past and an uncertain future, the Dolores remains a river worthy of the serious angler's attention. We hope the pool-management concept that has kept the river a viable trout fishery since 1990 will continue to be successful. The fat rainbows and browns that hide in the river's runs and pools are worth protecting.

UPPER CANYONS OF THE DOLORES RIVER

Managed by: San Juan National Forest
Access by: Vehicle, foot, and mountain bike
Altitude: 6,200 to 10,500 feet
Type of Water: Freestone stream, meadow water
Best Times: July to September
Hatches: Mayflies, caddisflies
Maps: San Juan National Forest; USGS Dolores West, Boggy Draw, Stoner, Wallace Ranch, Orphan Butte, Rico, Nipple Mountain, Clyde Lake, Dolores Peak, and Mount Wilson 7.5' quadrangles

The Dolores River is best known for its tailwater fishery below McPhee Reservoir, but in its upper reaches the river has an ample supply of mountain fishing to offer. Two branches, the main Dolores and the West Dolores, drain the high country below Mount Wilson and Lizard Head Pass in the western San Juan Mountains. It is an area rich in minerals and with a long history of mining that has created a mix of public and private land not found on many other southern Colorado rivers. Although the fishing is not as well known as on nearby streams, the upper Dolores does offer uncrowded streams amid some of the best scenery in the San Juans outside the Weminuche Wilderness.

The Dolores River heads below Lizard Head Pass and flows to the southwest through the mining town of Rico to enter McPhee Reservoir at the town of Dolores. Except for the uppermost miles, the entire river is paralleled by Colorado 145. From Durango, reach Colorado 145 by taking U.S. 160 west about 28 miles to Mancos. Turn right onto Colorado 184 and continue northwest 18 miles to Colorado 145. Turn right and you can follow the river about 50 miles. The West Dolores is off Colorado 145 on Forest Road 535, which loops

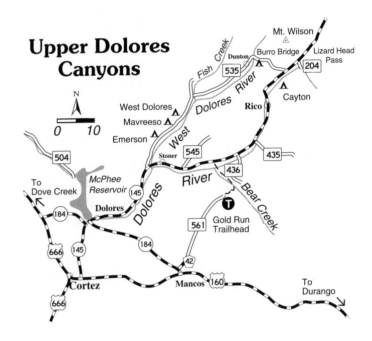

Upper Dolores Canyons

along the West Dolores and returns to Colorado 145. The lower end of Forest Road 535 is 16 miles north of Dolores, and the upper end of the road is about 8 miles below Lizard Head Pass, providing access to about 35 miles of river.

The closest large town to the upper Dolores is Cortez, 20 miles south of McPhee Dam. Cortez has a wide variety of services and lodging. Closer to the river, limited services are offered at Dolores and Rico. Numerous Forest Service campgrounds are located along the forks of the river.

On both forks the mix of public and private land makes angling a bit tricky. Most private land is clearly posted. Consult the San Juan National Forest map to get an overview of the land ownership boundaries along the rivers.

On the main Dolores public access is found just above McPhee Reservoir and through the town of Dolores. From

Dolores to Rico the river is entirely on private land except for short stretches at Stoner and a mile downstream from the Priest Gulch Trailhead, which is about 11 miles south of Rico. From 2 miles north of Rico to the headwaters, the Dolores lies within San Juan National Forest. Close to Lizard Head Pass, the Dolores turns east away from the highway and is reached by the rough Forest Road 204 and the East Fork Trail.

On the West Dolores, locally known as "the West Fork," landownership comes in blocks. Most public access surrounds the national forest campgrounds of Emerson, Mavreeso, and West Dolores. Watch carefully for posted land in this area. Above Dunton, the river stays on Forest Service land.

The lower portions of the Dolores forks are freestone waters flowing through broad canyons, but there is a good mix of pocket water and some long runs. The riverbanks are forested with conifers except at the lower end of the main branch. The rivers range from twenty to thirty feet in width, decreasing in size to become small meadow streams near the headwaters below Mount Wilson. In the canyons the rivers have moderately high gradients, and the West Dolores has a lower gradient and is easier to fish than the main Dolores. In the upper meadows both are small streams only a couple of feet across, making for challenging fly fishing.

The forks are wide enough to permit easy casting from within the streams. Hip boots will be sufficient for early- and late-season angling, and wet wading is pleasant throughout the summer. The rocky bottom can be slick, so bring appropriate footwear: Felt-soled wading shoes are best.

Anglers will find brown, brook, and rainbow trout in both forks of the Dolores. Fish are small, averaging 6 to 10 inches in the upper rivers near Lizard Head Pass and in the wilderness. Lower down in the canyons trout are larger, ranging from 10 to 14 inches, with a few rare larger fish. No special regulations are in effect on the West Dolores or the main Dolores.

As with most freestone mountain waters, trout in the upper Dolores are opportunistic feeders. Use a fly that is easy to see in choppy water, and one that you have confidence in. Because the fish in these streams don't see a lot of anglers, you can keep it simple. Royal Wulffs, Renegades, and the House and Lot Variant in sizes 12 to 16 will see you through most situations on the forks. Trout hold in the deep water of pockets and pools and any place where they can receive some protection from fast currents. Work in close to the fish, keeping casts as short as possible, and keeping most of the fly line off the water.

Two tributaries to the Dolores deserve mention. Fish Creek enters the West Dolores about 12 miles above Highway 145. Forest Road 726 passes through a mile of private land to reach the Fish Creek State Wildlife Area. Here and in the national forest above the Fish Creek Trail parallels the stream for about 6 miles. The stream is small, less than ten feet in width, and flows through alternately open and brushy meadows. Anglers will find small rainbows and browns from 6 to 10 inches, with some browns up to 14 inches.

Bear Creek is a major tributary of the main Dolores, joining the river about 9 miles east of Stoner. Access to the river is by trail only. A trailhead for Trail 607 is located on Highway 145 but is difficult to find. The trail first passes through private land, so stay on the designated path in this area. Upper Bear Creek is reached out of Mancos on County Road 42 and Forest Road 561, off Highway 184. Hike in to Bear Creek from the Gold Run Trailhead about 19 miles from Mancos. The trail drops steeply down to the river: Allow forty-five minutes to get down and twice that to make the challenging climb back.

Bear Creek is a small but fine stream holding nice brown, rainbow, and cutthroat trout. Angling for these fish is restricted to artificial flies and lures only for the entire stream, and a bag and possession limit of two fish is in effect.

11

IMPORTANT AQUATIC INSECTS OF SOUTHERN COLORADO

One of the unique attractions of fly fishing is that its practitioners can immerse themselves in the sport at many levels. You can dive in so deeply that you feel like an *Epeorus* mayfly nymph clinging to a rock in a swift mountain stream, or you can take a more casual approach. No aspect of the sport demonstrates this as vividly as the matter of aquatic insects. Some anglers choose to make bugs a major sidelight of the sport, becoming amateur aquatic entomologists. They conduct stream surveys of bugs, bringing magnifying glasses and sampling nets to the water along with rods and reels. At home, they study insects and learn to identify each species they find in their local waters. On the other hand, many equally successful anglers possess only enough knowledge to determine when to fish a dry mayfly pattern instead of a stonefly.

By no means is it necessary to know the Latin names of aquatic insects in order to successfully fish the waters of southern Colorado. Most trout in high-mountain streams are opportunistic feeders and will take anything that floats by. Anglers will commonly find that during a single hour patterns as diverse as a Joe's Hopper and a size 16 Parachute Ginger Dun will catch fish. However, at certain times of the season

Although most trout in southern Colorado are opportunistic feeders, fly patterns that match the insects on the water can, at certain times and places, enhance your chances for success. (Photograph by Craig Martin.)

and the day, or in certain places, trout will feed selectively. The fish will single out a particular insect, or even a specific stage of the insect's life cycle, and refuse all others. At such times, only anglers who can determine which insect the trout are taking will find fish tugging at the ends of their lines.

Each bit of knowledge of insects and their habitats can contribute to success on the water. At a minimum, anglers should be able to distinguish between the major groups of insects that serve as important food sources for trout: mayflies, stoneflies, caddisflies, midges, and terrestrials. The ability to determine what trout are taking begins simply by learning to take the time to observe events on and around the water. The ability to recognize species of insect enhances the angler's ability to anticipate and predict hatches on specific streams.

A large part of the literature of fly fishing is devoted to insects and their relationship to trout. Anglers who wish to learn more about trout food sources should seek out a few of the basic references such as Patrick McCafferty's treatise *Aquatic Entomology* (Jones & Bartlett, 1983), Dave Whitlock's excellent *Guide to Aquatic Trout Foods* (Nick Lyons Books, 1982), Rick Hafele and Dave Hughes's comprehensive *Western Hatches* (Frank Amato Publishers, 1981), and Gary La-Fontaine's *Caddisflies* (Nick Lyons Books, 1980).

The following list of aquatic insects of southern Colorado was compiled from reference materials and field surveys. The list is not meant to be a complete catalog of species but rather identifies the major insects found on the waters of the area. The approximate range of each insect is given by watershed and not by individual stream. Anglers who frequently fish southern Colorado should know how to recognize these insects. Use this list to help you identify the insects you find, and to predict when hatches might occur.

Mayflies

Scientific Name: *Baetis bicaudatus*, *Baetis tricaudatus*
Common Name: Blue-winged olive
Watersheds: Rio Grande, San Juan, Piedra, Los Pinos, Animas, La Plata, Dolores
Habitat: Riffles, runs, pools
Hatch: June to July (*B. tricaudatus*), heaviest in late fall (*B. bicaudatus*)
Time of Day: Midday
Patterns: Nymph, Pheasant Tail #18–24; adult, Blue-Winged Olive #18–24

Scientific Name: *Callibaetis americanus*
Common Name: Speckle-winged quill
Watersheds: Rio Grande, San Juan, Los Pinos, Animas
Habitat: Lakes, ponds, slow-moving streams

Hatch: June to September
Time of Day: Morning to afternoon
Patterns: Nymph, Timberline #12–16, Gold-Ribbed Hare's Ear #12–16; adult, Light Cahill #14–18

Scientific Name: *Drunella coloradensis (Ephemerella coloradensis)*
Common Name: Slate-winged dun
Watersheds: Rio Grande, San Juan, Piedra, Animas, La Plata, Dolores
Habitat: Swift streams
Hatch: July to August
Time of Day: Mid- to late morning
Patterns: Nymph, Dark Olive Hare's Ear #12–14; adult, Green Drake #12–14, Green Wulff #12–14

Scientific Name: *Drunella doddsi (Ephemerella doddsi), Drunella grandis (Ephemerella grandis)*
Common Name: Western green drake
Watersheds: Rio Grande, San Juan, Piedra, Animas, Dolores
Habitat: Swift streams
Hatch: June to late August
Time of Day: Late morning to early afternoon
Patterns: Nymph, Dark Olive Hare's Ear #10–14; adult, Green Drake Wulff #10–14, Green Drake Comparadun #10–14

Scientific Name: *Ephemerella inermis, Ephemerella infrequens*
Common Name: Pale morning dun
Watersheds: Rio Grande, San Juan, Piedra, Animas, La Plata, Dolores
Habitat: Stream edges
Hatch: July to August
Time of Day: Mid- to late morning

Patterns: Nymph, Dark Hare's Ear Nymph #16–18, Pheasant Tail #16–18; adult, Parachute Light Cahill #16–18, PMD Comparadun #16–18

Scientific Name: *Serratella tibialis, Serratella micheneri*
Common Name: Western red quill
Watersheds: Rio Grande, San Juan, Animas
Habitat: Swift water
Hatch: Late June to early September
Time of Day: Midday
Patterns: Nymph, Gold-Ribbed Hare's Ear #14–18; adult, Brown Wulff #14–18, Red Quill #14–18

Scientific Name: *Epeorus albertae, Epeorus longimanus*
Common Name: Pink lady, western gordon quill
Watersheds: Rio Grande, San Juan, Piedra, Los Pinos, Animas, La Plata, Dolores
Habitat: Fast streams, riffles
Hatch: July and August
Time of Day: Midmorning through early afternoon
Patterns: Nymph, Gold-Ribbed Hare's Ear #14–18, AP Beaver #14–18; adult, Grizzly Wulff #14–18, Pink Lady #16–18

Scientific Name: *Heptagenia elegantula, Heptagenia solitaria*
Common Name: Western pale evening dun
Watersheds: San Juan, Piedra, Los Pinos, Animas, La Plata, Dolores
Habitat: Edges of riffles and pocket water
Hatch: Mid-June to mid-August
Time of Day: Late afternoon and evening
Patterns: Nymph, Gold-Ribbed Hare's Ear #14–16; adult, Light Cahill #14–16, Cream Comparadun #14–16

Scientific Name: *Rhithrogena hageni, Rhithrogena robusta*
Common Name: Red quill, march brown
Watersheds: Rio Grande, San Juan, Piedra, Los Pinos, Animas, La Plata, Dolores
Habitat: Fast currents in small and large streams
Hatch: Early July to mid-August
Time of Day: Morning
Patterns: Nymph, Pheasant Tail #12–14; adult, Red Quill #12–18, Brown Wulff #12–16

Scientific Name: *Tricorythodes minutus*
Common Name: White-winged Trico
Watersheds: Rio Grande
Habitat: Slow water in streams
Hatch: Mid-June to early September
Time of Day: Early to midmorning
Patterns: Nymph, Pheasant Tail #20–24; adult, Poly-wing Spinner #20–24

Stoneflies

Scientific Name: *Capnia* spp. (5–6 species)
Common Name: Little winter stonefly
Watersheds: Rio Grande, San Juan, Piedra, Los Pinos, Animas, La Plata, Dolores
Dates of Hatch: January to June
Time of Hatch: Sporadic
Patterns: Nymph, AP Black #14–18; adult, Little Black Stonefly #12–14

Scientific Name: *Sweltsa coloradensis, Sweltsa lamba*
Common Name: Little green stonefly
Watersheds: Rio Grande, San Juan, Piedra, Los Pinos, Animas, La Plata, Dolores
Dates of Hatch: Mid-April to August

Time of Hatch: Late afternoon and evening
Patterns: Nymph, Pheasant Tail Soft-Hackle #16–18, Partridge and Green Soft-Hackle #16–18; adult, Green Bucktail Caddis #18–20, Lime Trude #14–18

Scientific Name: *Hesperoperla pacifica (Acroneuria californica)*
Common Name: Golden stonefly
Watersheds: Rio Grande, San Juan, Piedra, Los Pinos, Animas, La Plata
Dates of Hatch: June to August
Time of Hatch: Late afternoon and evening
Patterns: Nymph, Light Brooks Stone #2–8 , Kaufmann Stone #2–8; adult, Bird's Stonefly #4–8, Stimulator #8–12

Scientific Name: *Isoperla mormona* (about 5 other species)
Common Name: Western yellow stonefly, yellow sally
Watersheds: Rio Grande, San Juan, Piedra, Los Pinos, Animas, La Plata, Dolores
Dates of Hatch: May to August
Time of Hatch: Late evening
Patterns: Nymph, Little Yellow Stone Nymph #12–14 (Rosborough), Partridge-and-Yellow Soft-Hackle #12–14; adult, Yellow Bucktail Caddis #12–14, Stimulator #12–16, Little Yellow Stone #12–14 (Rosborough)

Scientific Name: *Pteronarcella badia*
Common Name: Small salmon fly
Watersheds: Rio Grande, San Juan, Piedra, Los Pinos, Animas, La Plata, Dolores
Dates of Hatch: June to July
Time of Hatch: Late afternoon and evening
Patterns: Nymph, Montana Stone #2–8 (Brooks), Kaufmann Stone #2–8, Box Canyon Stone #2–8 (Barker); adult, Royal Stimulator #8–14

Scientific Name: *Pteronarcys californica*
Common Name: Salmon fly
Watersheds: Rio Grande, San Juan, Piedra, Los Pinos, Animas, La Plata, Dolores
Dates of Hatch: June to July
Time of Hatch: Late afternoon and evening
Patterns: Nymph, Brooks Stone #2–8, Kaufmann Stone #2–8, Bitch Creek Nymph #2–8; adult: Bird's Stonefly #4–8, Stimulator #6–10

Caddisflies

Scientific Name: *Brachycentrus americanus, Brachycentrus occidentalis*
Common Name: American grannom
Watersheds: Rio Grande
Dates of Hatch: June through September
Time of Hatch: Late afternoon and evening
Patterns: Larva, Cased Caddis #10–16; pupa, Partridge Soft-Hackle #12–14; adult, Elk Hair Caddis #10–16

Scientific Name: *Glossosoma* spp. (2–3 species)
Common Name: Saddlecase maker
Watersheds: San Juan, Piedra, Los Pinos, Animas, La Plata, Dolores
Dates of Hatch: June through September
Time of Hatch: Late afternoon
Patterns: Pupa, Cream Soft-Hackle #14–18; adult, Elk Hair Caddis #12–16, Peacock Caddis #12–16

Scientific Name: *Hydropsyche cockerelli, Hydropsyche occidentalis*
Common Name: Spotted sedge
Watersheds: Rio Grande, San Juan, Piedra, Los Pinos, Animas, La Plata, Dolores
Dates of Hatch: June through September

Time of Hatch: Late afternoon
Patterns: Larva, Cream Caddis Larva #12–16; pupa, Cream Sparkle Pupa #12–16 (LaFontaine), March Brown Soft-Hackle #12–16; adult, Elk Hair Caddis #12–16, Goddard Caddis #12–16

Scientific Name: *Rhyacophila* spp. (5–6 species)
Common Name: Green rock worm
Watersheds: Rio Grande, San Juan, Piedra, Los Pinos, Animas, La Plata, Dolores
Dates of Hatch: May through September
Time of Hatch: Afternoon
Patterns: Larva, Rhyacophila Caddis Larva #10–16 (Kaufmann); pupa, Partridge and Green Soft-Hackle #10–16; adult, Dark Bucktail Caddis #10–14, Olive Elk Hair Caddis #12–16

Diptera

Family: Tipulidae
Common Name: Craneflies
Watersheds: Throughout southern Colorado
Dates of Hatch: April through October
Patterns: Larva, Muskrat #8–10 (Rosborough), Western Cranefly Larva #10–12 (Schwiebert), Woolly Worm #10–12; adult, Ginger Spider #10–16, Ginger Variant #10–16, Darbee Crane Fly #8–10

Family: Culicidae
Common Name: Mosquitos
Watersheds: Throughout southern Colorado
Dates of Hatch: June to September
Patterns: Larva, Mosquito Larva #14–20; adult, Adams #14–20, Mosquito #14–20

Family: Chironomidae
Common Name: Midges
Watersheds: Throughout southern Colorado
Dates of Hatch: All year
Patterns: Larva, Brassie #18–24, Dave's Midge Larva #18–24; pupa, Chironomid Pupa #18–24 (Kaufmann in brown, black, olive, gray), Emerging Pupa #18–24 (Whitlock in black, brown, green); adult, Parachute Midge Cluster #14–18, Fore-and-Aft Midge Cluster #14–18, Griffith's Gnat #18–24

APPENDIX

List of Sources
for Additional Information

Backcountry Angler
350 Pagosa Avenue
Pagosa Springs, CO 81147
(970) 264-4202

Colorado Division of Wildlife
Monte Vista Office
722 South County Road
Monte Vista, CO 81144
(719) 852-4783

Columbine Ranger District
701 Camino del Rio
Durango, CO 81301
(970) 247-4874

Conejos Peak Ranger District
21461 State Highway 285
La Jara, CO 81140
(719) 274-5193

Creede–Mineral County Chamber of Commerce
P.O. Box 580
Creede, CO 81130
(800) 327-2102

Creede Ranger District
3rd and Creede Avenue
Creede, CO 81130
(719) 658-2556

Dolores Ranger District
100 North 6th
Dolores, CO 81323
(970) 882-7296

Duranglers Flies and Supplies
801B Main Avenue
Durango, CO 81301
(970) 385-4081

Durango Chamber of Commerce
P.O. Box 2587
Durango, CO 81302
(800) 525-8855

Pagosa Ranger District
P.O. Box 310
Pagosa Springs, CO 81147
(970) 264-2268

Pagosa Springs Area Chamber of Commerce
P.O. Box 787
Pagosa Springs, CO 81147
(800) 252-2204

Pine Ranger District
367 South Pearl Street
Bayfield, CO 81122
(970) 884-2512

Rio Grande National Forest
U.S. Forest Service
810 Grand Avenue
Del Norte, CO 81132
(719) 657-3321

San Juan National Forest
U.S. Forest Service
701 Camino del Rio
Durango, CO 81301
(970) 247-4874

Southern Ute Natural Resource Division
P.O. Box 737
Ignacio, CO 81137
(970) 563-0125

Sources on the Internet

Colorado Fishing
http://www.ofps.ucar.edu/~john/fish/

CompuServe Fly Fishing Forum
Outdoors Forum/Fishing Forum

Durango Downtown
http://www.creativelinks.com/

Internet Fly Fishing Newsgroup
rec.outdoors.fishing.fly

Rocky Mountain Fly Fishing Center
http://www.xmission.com/~gastown/flyfishing/index.html

Virtual Fly Shop
http://www.flyshop.com

INDEX